Living SERENITY

The Serenity Prayer and Scripture

Deborah Galasso

5 Fold Media
Visit us at www.5foldmedia.com

Living Serenity

Published by 5 Fold Media, LLC
www.5foldmedia.com

For bulk orders of twenty (20) or more books, contact 5 Fold Media by email sales@5foldmedia.com or call 315-314-6480.

The identity of some individuals referred to in this book may have been changed to protect anonymity. All others are used with consent.

ISBN: 978-1-936578-79-5
Library of Congress Control Number: 2013951320

The Serenity Prayer

God, grant me the serenity
to accept the things I cannot change,
the courage to change the things I can,
and the wisdom to know the difference.
Living one day at a time,
enjoying one moment at a time,
accepting hardship as a pathway to peace,
taking as Jesus did, this sinful world as it is,
not as I would have it,
trusting that You will make all things right
if I surrender to Your will,
so that I may be reasonably happy in this life
and supremely happy with You forever in the next.
Amen.

-Reinhold Niebuhr

Contents

Introduction

Undoubtedly when Reinhold Niebuhr sat down to pen the words to a prayer to accompany an ordinary Sunday sermon he was giving in a small farming village in Massachusetts, he had no idea that the prayer would come to be known as "The Serenity Prayer." Had he lived to see it, he might have been more than a little embarrassed and amused, given his humble nature, to know that the editors of the *World Almanac* selected his prayer as one of the ten most memorable quotes by Americans in the last one hundred years.[1] And although the award was based on the prayer's popularity, the prayer could have easily been honored for another reason—the extent to which those words had so powerfully influenced the lives of millions of struggling people. When put into practice, the principles embodied in this simple prayer can profoundly change the manner in which we approach life, and subsequently result in an enduring sense of serenity. I can say this with complete confidence because I was one of those millions of struggling people whose life was changed by the Serenity Prayer.

From the time I was a young child and throughout the majority of my adulthood, I struggled with fear and anxiety. In my twenties I chose the self-medication solution for my escalating fear problem, which ultimately added addiction to my particular medley of problems. As debilitating as that was, it was the addiction that led me to my first recovery group and the Serenity Prayer. So in addition to being a book about developing serenity through the practice of the principles contained in the Serenity Prayer, this book is also about my understanding of the processes of addiction and recovery. As used in this book, the term *addiction* refers to an unhealthy pattern of behavior associated with the compulsive use of a substance or process which results in physiological or psychological dependency. The term *recovery* refers to the ongoing process of regaining a balanced, healthy approach to life, of which serenity is a component.

Because I am a Christian who is recovering from the effects of the disease of addiction, this book is also about integrating the principles of the Serenity Prayer with the truth of Scripture. Bringing my Christian faith into the process of recovery is particularly important to me because decades ago when I first began my journey of recovery from addiction, it was necessary to go outside my church to find the specific help I needed. Although I found it difficult to believe that in a church with hundreds of members I was the only person struggling with an addiction, no one talked openly about addiction, and at that time there were no small groups within my church which addressed this problem. When I turned to secular twelve-step groups, I was both surprised and grateful to find that there were many other Christians there with whom I could share the journey of recovery. As a result of those groups, I began to recover and experience serenity, but I continued to wish that there was a way to openly integrate the teachings of my recovery program with the truth of Scripture. So in addition to being a book about serenity, it is also a book about Christ-centered recovery.

I realize that a book that seeks to bridge the gap between traditional recovery programs and Christianity will be viewed as controversial by many. Some in the Christian community will reject the notion that "real Christians" struggle with anything, let alone an addiction problem that requires an ongoing program of recovery. This group tends to emphasize deliverance to the exclusion of process. While it is true that God can, and often does, dramatically remove a person's desire for an addiction, there still remains in most individuals the need for lifestyle change and renewed thinking, which is exactly the purpose of a program of recovery. This idea is supported by Paul, who talked about transformation from unhealthy patterns of behavior being accomplished by the renewing of one's thoughts, which implies a process rather than an event (Romans 12:2). By failing to provide resources for ongoing recovery from addictive problems, the church unwittingly supports the denial that keeps transformation at bay.

On the other side of the coin are a number of secular twelve-step recovery purists who insist that any mention of Jesus Christ constitutes religiosity, violates program traditions, and therefore has no place in a bona fide recovery group. This position is interesting in light of the fact that the concept of each individual determining their own understanding of God is a key component of the twelve steps of recovery. The traditions established in secular twelve-step groups exist to provide a framework of consistency across groups, unity among members, and clarity of purpose that are important to the preservation of the groups. However, it is not entirely unreasonable to believe that one can identify one's "Higher Power" as Jesus Christ without entering into a discussion of specific religious tenets that would violate program traditions.

While one group may find the ideas presented in this book to be too secular, the other group may find them to be too doctrinal. However, this book was not written for either of these two groups. Instead, it was written for a group of people commonly referred to both inside and outside the church as "those people"—those who struggle; those who have addiction problems; those who have emotional problems; those acquainted with the insanity of repeating the same behaviors again and again while hoping for different results; those who strive to look good on the outside, yet feel like a mess on the inside; those who don a pretend smile that says "everything is okay," when their lives are actually spinning out of control; those who are doing their best to hide the awful truth about themselves from themselves as well as others; those who question whether or not they are Christians because of their struggle; those who have tried praying harder and reading their Bibles more, yet find they still need something more.

If you, like me, are one of "those people," it is my hope that you will realize as you read through this book that there is a path that leads to serenity. It is the kind of serenity that I refer to as "living serenity." Living serenity is both an entity as well as an action. It is an entity in that serenity is continually evolving and growing, moment by moment, and in that respect can be considered "living." Living serenity is an action in that it is the direction our lives can take when we decide to seriously and persistently practice, that is live out, the principles found in the Serenity Prayer.

In the chapters that follow, the various ideas and principles contained in the prayer are examined in depth. Beginning with chapter two, each chapter is divided into three sections. The first section explores a particular word, phrase, or principle contained in the Serenity Prayer and examines it in light of what Scripture teaches. The second section is the "...and Me" section in which I share my personal story along with examples of how I have applied the prayer's principles to the conditions which contribute to, and are associated with, addiction. The third section is the "...and You" section which provides questions for you to consider in order to explore your own struggles as well as apply the prayer's principles to your life. Also included in this section are additional scriptural references which will further your understanding of what the Bible says about the chapter topic. Although space has been provided for recording your responses, if it is your intent to complete an in-depth study of the Scriptures included in the "And You" sections, it is recommended that a separate notebook be used to allow for additional space for writing. While this book is intended to be used by individuals, it can also serve as the basis for a weekly Bible study for recovery groups.

I do not profess to be an expert on theology, prayer, or Scripture, nor an authority on serenity and recovery. I am simply a follower of Christ as well as a recovering person who wishes to share my experience, strength, and hope. It is my sincere desire that this book will serve as a tool which furthers your walk with Christ, enriches your journey of recovery, and leads you to living serenity.

Chapter One: A Brief History of the Serenity Prayer

Over the course of many years of working a twelve-step program, there have been a number of tools that have aided my recovery. But if I had to choose the one which has had the greatest impact on assisting me to develop serenity, I would select the Serenity Prayer. While the twelve steps have provided a vital framework for self-change, it takes time to practice them long enough to reap their benefits. When I began using the Serenity Prayer, I felt the benefits immediately. For someone previously used to achieving speedy results through self-medication, this alone was quite rewarding!

The reaction that I had to the power of this prayer was not unlike that of Bill Wilson, the cofounder of Alcoholics Anonymous (AA). He was introduced to the prayer early in 1942 by a New York AA member who saw it quoted in an obituary. The prayer as it appeared in the obituary read: "God grant us the serenity to accept the things we cannot change, courage to change the things we can, and wisdom to know the difference." Wilson was struck by both the wisdom and the power contained in the prayer, commenting, "Never had we seen so much AA in so few words."[2]

It was suggested that the prayer be printed on wallet-sized cards and sent out with every piece of outgoing mail from AA's home office. Wilson was amazed at the speed with which the prayer gained popularity among the AA membership. At the time it was first printed by AA, authorship of the prayer was unknown to Wilson.[3] Eventually, authorship of the prayer would be attributed to Reinhold Niebuhr.

Niebuhr was a prominent American Protestant theologian who lived from June 21, 1892 to June 1, 1971. Following in the footsteps of his father, who was a pastor, he earned his master's degree from Yale University in 1914 and was ordained the following year. He was assigned to a church in Detroit whose congregation of one hundred grew to six hundred during the first six years of his pastorate. This phenomenal rate of growth was due in part to his captivating style of preaching. In 1928 he became professor of Christian ethics at New York Union Theological Seminary where he eventually served as dean. In addition to being a prolific author, he was outspoken on a wide variety of social and political issues. He was unafraid to take controversial or unpopular stands, such as opposing the labor practices of Henry Ford or challenging the wisdom of American pacifism in the face of Nazi aggression in Europe.[4]

In spite of his many accomplishments, Reinhold Niebuhr is best remembered for authoring what has come to be known as the Serenity Prayer. According to his daughter, Elisabeth Sifton, Niebuhr used the prayer during a sermon at Heath Union Church in 1943. The prayer began to be circulated through the efforts of Howard Chandler Robbins, who was a friend of Niebuhr's. He was so impressed with the prayer that he obtained Niebuhr's permission to have the prayer included in a booklet for army chaplains and servicemen that was published by the Federal Council of Churches in 1944.[5] The booklet was distributed by the USO to hundreds of thousands of servicemen.[6]

Interestingly, Niebuhr never intended his prayer to become the popular tool for self-improvement into which it has evolved today. The prayer as he originally wrote it was: "God give us grace to accept with serenity the things that cannot be changed, courage to change the things that should be changed, and the wisdom to distinguish the one from the other." The original wording supports the idea that it was written to be a communal prayer which reflected Niebuhr's convictions regarding social injustice. Although Niebuhr did not approve of the fact that the wording of his prayer had been altered over the years, he resisted copyrighting the prayer because he could not conceive of using prayer to profit monetarily.[7] It wasn't until 1951 that he finally published his prayer in one of his magazine columns. That version read: "God, give us the serenity to accept what cannot changed; give us the courage to change what should be changed; give us the wisdom to distinguish one from the other." While one Niebuhr biographer wrote that the prayer was copyrighted in 1962 and used in a series of graduation cards,[8] Niebuhr's daughter indicated in her book about the Serenity Prayer that it had never been copyrighted.[9]

In recent years, authorship of the prayer has been called into question because of conflicting timelines regarding when the prayer was written. The accounts of the prayer appearing in a 1942 obituary cannot be confirmed and are seemingly at odds with the belief of Niebuhr's daughter that he wrote the prayer in the summer of 1943. Niebuhr's wife, Ursula, also believed that he penned the prayer early in the 1940s. However, Fred Shapiro, who edited the *Yale Book of Quotations*, has uncovered a variety of published narratives containing lines similar to those in Niebuhr's prayer by various authors from 1936 to 1941. Niebuhr's daughter has responded to this discovery by pointing out that her father's prayers were used orally in his sermons all over the country before they were published by him and that this could explain how these lines began showing up in print prior to the early 1940s.[10] In 2009, Stephen Goranson, a researcher at Duke University, uncovered a version of the Serenity Prayer in a 1937 publication which credited Niebuhr as the author.[11] Niebuhr always asserted his authorship of the prayer, but also left room for doubt. His response to repeated questions regarding his authorship was to note that all works of literature had their roots in the past, and so it was possible that there could be subconscious traces of the past in his.[12]

The greater unknown regarding the origin of the Serenity Prayer is who authored the version that is being used in this book. This version reads:

> "God, grant me the serenity to accept the things I cannot change, the courage to change the things I can, and the wisdom to know the difference. Living one day at a time; enjoying one moment at a time; accepting hardship as a pathway to peace;

taking as Jesus did, this sinful world as it is, not as I would have it; trusting that You will make all things right if I surrender to Your will, so that I may be reasonably happy in this life and supremely happy with You forever in the next."

I was first introduced to this version when I attended a church-based twelve-step group during the 1990s. Having been in traditional twelve-step groups for a number of years, I was familiar with the beginning line of the prayer and had found it extremely useful to my recovery. While the original line concisely addressed the goals of addiction recovery, these additional lines encapsulated the essence of the teachings of Jesus. Practiced together, they provided a powerful tool for increasing spiritual growth and serenity.

Authorship of this version of the prayer has been attributed to Reinhold Niebuhr, but that is incorrect as only the first part of the prayer, which has undergone many revisions along the way, resembles the prayer originally penned by him. The second part of the prayer never appeared in his published version, nor did it appear in his daughter's book about the prayer. Obviously at some point in time, someone added these lines to the prayer. The question of who authored these words and when they were added to the original prayer is a mystery. I have researched this to the best of my ability, but have been unable to determine the answer. I consulted both Mr. Shapiro and Mr. Goranson because I knew that they had researched this prayer extensively through a variety of searchable historic text collections; both indicated that they had not encountered this extended version of the prayer in any of their research.[13, 14]

Regardless of this mystery, the version of the prayer that we are about to explore contains the same wisdom and power as all the other versions which have been inspiring serenity seekers for over eight decades.

Chapter Two: God

It *all* begins with God: all life, all growth, all serenity. The greatest book ever written begins with this truth: "In the beginning God..." (Genesis 1:1). All beginnings, including those related to making positive changes in our lives, start with Him. If we desire to live a life characterized by serenity, the most logical place to begin is with God.

Too often in life, we are tempted to look for serenity in all the wrong places: relationships, success, and money, to name just a few. We think that if we can find the right relationship, or land a better job, it will bring us peace. We mistakenly believe that if we had just a little more money to make our lives a bit more comfortable we would feel at ease. While these circumstances have the potential to contribute to a more fulfilling life, they won't necessarily satisfy the longing we all share for deep and abiding tranquility.

There was a time when I didn't understand that the serenity I craved inside could never come from the outside world. In my ignorance, I turned to things that initially seemed to bring peace but in reality were harmful and eventually resulted in an addiction that left me spiritually bankrupt. I misperceived the temporary comfort they provided as serenity. What I actually needed was a serenity that the world couldn't give. I needed something greater than relationships, success, money, chemicals, and even myself. The "something greater" that ultimately brought serenity to my life wasn't some "thing," it was someone: God.

To understand God's role with regard to serenity, we must first understand that the world we inhabit is broken. It isn't the world God intended for us when He originally created the human race. God's intention was for all people to live in a perfect world characterized by serenity flowing from an experience of complete harmony with God and others. We wouldn't need to find serenity because it would be the ongoing state in which we lived. Unfortunately when sin entered the picture, the intended perfection was shattered, resulting in disrupted relationship with God, self, and others.

As a Christian, I had heard this explanation a million times and yet failed to appreciate the extent of sin's damage. I grew up thinking the world was okay: I was the only thing that was broken and in need of a Savior. I didn't grasp the reality that when sin arrived, everything in creation changed, not just the spiritual state of people. Scripture tells us that all of creation cries out for restoration (Romans 8:20-22). The balance and harmony with which God had originally endowed the world shifted drastically when sin entered the picture.

The world is broken and none of us are left untouched by that fact. Children are abused; poverty takes its toll; prejudice rears its ugly head; pain and hardship abound. Over the course of our lifetimes, each of us will be affected by that brokenness in a variety of ways, regardless of what we do or fail to do. Living a life characterized by serenity can never depend on the absence of brokenness.

As foundational as the understanding of this idea was to finding serenity, there was one that was even more important. To experience living serenity in a broken world, I would have to become acquainted with the God in charge of beginnings. This was news to me. I thought I *did* know God. After all, I was taken to church from the time I was born. I learned all the Bible stories about Him, sang all the songs about Him, and committed my life to Him at an early age. It wasn't until I landed in my first twelve-step group that I became aware that I didn't truly know God. What I knew was a God of my understanding—a God whose perfect character had become tainted by my experiences in a broken, imperfect world.

The concept of God I developed was to a large extent shaped and molded by exposure to religious training during my childhood which focused almost exclusively on sin, punishment, and the need to fear

God. As a result of this lopsided orientation, I definitely feared God, but it was the knee-knocking kind of fear, not the reverent kind. I viewed God as a punitive Being who demanded perfection. I was taught that sin was something that I could and should avoid, lest I invite God's punishment. I had difficulty reconciling the idea that God loved me but hated sin. My young mind translated this idea into the belief that "God hates me when I sin"; and since I couldn't stop sinning, I believed God needed to punish me to "help" me with my sin problem.

I was confused by what I perceived the church's teachings to be: God loves me, but not when I sin; Christ died for all my sin, except the unconfessed ones; salvation was for eternity, unless at some point I committed the "unpardonable" sin. The fact that no one seemed to be able to describe, much less agree upon, just what that unpardonable sin was left me in quite a quandary! In spite of being told that "God is love," my life became dominated by shame and fear.

Additionally, my perception of God's character suffered from another misconception which is quite common—the tendency to project experiences with influential authority figures onto God. By teaching us to begin our prayers with "Our Father" (Matthew 6:9), Jesus was acknowledging the importance of being able to perceive the fatherly characteristics of God. While I needed to experience God as a heavenly Father, experiences with my earthly father prevented me from perceiving the paternal qualities of God's character. Having grown up with an angry, domineering, judgmental father who seemed arbitrary and impossible to please, I found it difficult to view God as benevolent and loving. Given these influences, God became someone to be avoided, not trusted. How could there be any experience of serenity with that perception?

The road to living serenity began when I discovered that my perceptions of God were not accurate. As I described to my first recovery group my reluctance to trust God, a very wise person turned to me and said, "Did you ever realize that you can throw out all the stuff you've ever been told or taught about God and start over? You can discover for yourself who He is instead." Discover God for myself? What a novel idea! If I had to pinpoint the exact moment when I began to find serenity, it would be the moment I decided to let God reveal Himself to me.

One way I chose to do this was to read about Him in His own words. I decided to set aside preconceived ideas and teachings and read through the Bible completely, aided not by Bible commentaries but only by the sincere desire to know Him. I must admit to experiencing a certain amount of dread as I approached the Old Testament. My recollection of it from sitting through eighteen years of Sunday sermons was that God was angry, vengeful, and punishing. Apparently, I was in good company when it came to this misconception. The great theologian, Martin Luther, once said, "If I could believe that God was not angry with me, I would stand on my head with joy."[15]

Imagine the surprise and joy I experienced when my biblical survey revealed a completely different picture of God—one in which the overall message was of His fierce love and unending desire for relationship with the people He had created. It was as though I was reading Scripture for the first time. I was especially struck by the fact that God described Himself as merciful, gracious, "slow to anger and filled with unfailing love and faithfulness" (Exodus 34:6). Throughout the Old Testament, God was described repeatedly as caring and compassionate. To be compassionate is to actively demonstrate concern for the suffering of another. I began to see that rather than wanting to punish me, He wanted to be my teacher, counselor, and guide (Psalm 32:8). He didn't expect me to be perfect and He wasn't after vengeance; on the contrary, He wanted to be a shield, refuge, and help for me (Psalms 7:10; 46:1; 54:4).

God's intentions toward me included "goodness and unfailing love" over the course of my whole life (Psalm 23:6). His character trait of graciousness meant that He would do for me what I could not do for myself. What a relief for an imperfect, serial sinner like me! Because He had a good future planned for me (Jeremiah 29:11), I could dare to hope. As I continued my journey through His story, my fear of Him was replaced by an appreciation and respect which moved me increasingly closer to trust. How could I fail to trust a God who loved so lavishly?

The potential for living a life characterized by living serenity began with a simple, honest request for God to reveal Himself to me. It is a request He will always honor because He "rewards those who sincerely seek Him" (Hebrews 11:6). The story of Rahab, a prostitute living in the doomed city of Jericho, demonstrates the lengths to which God will go in order to reach anyone who is seeking Him. Joshua sent the spies out on a military reconnaissance mission; God sent the spies out on a spiritual rescue mission. God already had a plan to capture Jericho—what He needed was a means of reaching the one person ready to make a declaration of belief in Him (Joshua 2:11).

God assures us that when we seek Him with a sincere heart, we will find Him (Jeremiah 29:13). Many people speak of "finding" God as though He is playing some cosmic game of hide and seek. The truth is that God isn't lost, so He doesn't need to be found. His thoughts are loftier than our thoughts (Isaiah 55:9), so He does not need to be understood. He instead needs to be known. He delights in replacing our inaccurate projections with knowledge of His true identity and character. Admitting our need to know Him and inviting Him to heal our distorted perceptions forms the foundation that allows us to begin to pray the Serenity Prayer in faith and trust.

"God" and Me

I can't for the life of me remember the name of that wise person who launched me on my mission to reevaluate my concept of God, but I remember the moment it happened as though it were yesterday. Had I been a cartoon character sitting in that recovery group that evening, a light bulb would have appeared above my head heralding the birth of a new and brilliant idea. Decades later as I recall that moment, I am filled with gratitude as I realize that the direction of my life was changed forever.

Before that moment, my life was dominated by fear and dread. I worried about everything. I couldn't turn to God with my doubts because of my distorted image of Him. My fear, as well as my inaccurate perceptions of God, diminished only as my relationship with Him increased. When I stopped trying to understand Him and instead focused on knowing Him; when I quit asking the "why" questions and instead asked the "who" questions; when I ceased hiding from Him and instead became willing to move toward Him, serenity began to replace the fear. Today, my concept of God is so vastly different that it's hard for me to believe that I was once so fearful of Him.

One particular moment when God revealed His character to me stands out above the rest. Wrestling with my inaccurate perceptions of God led to the need to examine my relationship with my father. Because my father was deceased, there could be no opportunity to discuss and resolve the misunderstandings of the past. Repairing my relationship with him was something that could only be done in my heart. One day while praying I began to grieve the unfulfilled longing for wholeness in my relationship with my father. I was kneeling prostrate on the floor while my daughter, who was five years old at the time, sat on the bed with her blanket, watching television. As I silently prayed, I quietly began to weep and tell God how desperately I needed Him to be not just my "heavenly Father," but to demonstrate a father's love in a tangible and personal way. At just that moment, my daughter walked over to me and dropped her blanket on top of me. As the warmth and weight of it encompassed my back and shoulders, it felt just like an embrace. In that moment, God demonstrated that He was indeed my loving Father and began to heal a relationship which I thought could not be repaired.

The quest to know God is never ending. My knowledge of Him is ever increasing and expanding as He continues to reveal Himself to me in new and different ways. There is no end to the ways in which He demonstrates His character to me. Much of the time it is through a Bible verse, often one I have read time and time again, yet at that particular moment I understand it in a new and revealing way. Sometimes it is through a conversation with a fellow believer who shares ways God is at work in her circumstances. At times it is through His creation as I realize the truth of the old hymn that says "He speaks to me everywhere."[16] More often than not, it is while I am sitting in one of my recovery groups listening to the miracles happening in the lives of others that I am reminded of who He is.

And who He is, is the God who never gave up on me and led me to that moment of spiritual awakening that changed my understanding of Him forever and became the beginning of my living serenity.

"God" and You

1. What is your perception of God? How has it changed over the course of your life?

2. How have your experiences with people influenced your perception of God? How have events and circumstances in your life influenced your perception of God?

3. Why is it important to have an accurate perception of who God is? How does your perception of God influence your recovery?

4. Read the following Scriptures and list the characteristics of God found in each. How have you experienced these attributes in your recovery? Which of these are you most in need of experiencing at this point in your recovery? (Deuteronomy 10:18; Deuteronomy 20:4; Psalm 9:9; Psalm 11:7; Psalm 18:2; Psalm 27:1; Psalm 145:9; Daniel 9:9; 2 Peter 3:9)

5. What do the following Scriptures reveal about God's attitude toward those who seek Him? (Psalm 9:10; Psalm 14:2; Isaiah 55:6; Jeremiah 29:13; Lamentations 3:25; Acts 17:27)

___

___

___

___

___

6. What do the following Scriptures relate about the benefits of seeking God? (Psalm 22:26; Psalm 34:10; Psalm 69:32; Psalm 70:4; Psalm 119:2; Amos 5:4)

___

___

___

___

___

7. What does Scripture indicate about God's understanding versus human understanding? (Job 36:26; Job 37:5; Proverbs 3:5; Isaiah 6:10; Isaiah 40:13-14, 28)

___

___

___

___

8. Read Romans 11:33-36. What is your reaction to Paul's description of God?

___

___

___

9. What idea from this chapter do you plan to put into practice?

___

___

___

___

Chapter Three: God Grant

The phrase "God grant" reminds me of an important spiritual truth: God is in control. While the focus of the Serenity Prayer is on God granting serenity, acceptance, courage, and wisdom, His ability to grant is actually unlimited. To pray the words, "God grant," is to acknowledge that everything in life comes through Him and by Him. Until I could accept the fact that God was in control, serenity remained elusive.

The theological term which refers to God's ability to be in control is called "sovereignty." Most of us are familiar with the term *sovereignty* as it applies to a government. The person who is sovereign is recognized as the head of state and has complete power and authority with regard to the affairs of state. With regard to God, the term *sovereign* means the "absolute right to govern all things as He chooses, without any limitations imposed by circumstances or human choices."[17] Quite simply, everything in creation is under His control. He isn't just the "higher power" referred to in twelve-step groups; He is the highest power. The only limitation on God is that He cannot act in ways that are inconsistent with His character.

The idea that God is in control of everything was one of the most foundational principles I had to come to terms with early in my recovery. It was a concept that was both reassuring and terrifying. I liked the idea of a loving, benevolent God being in control of the universe. I had paid lip service to that idea throughout my Christian walk. I say lip service because many of us who profess to be Christians say we believe that God is in control, yet we live our lives as though He were not. It is the difference between acknowledging the truth of a principle intellectually versus living out the truth of a principle experientially.

If I truly believed that God was in control, then that meant I wasn't, and I didn't like that idea quite as much. How could I live a happy and serene life if I wasn't in control? Not that my attempts to control things were all that successful. I certainly wasn't getting the results for which I had been hoping. Significant others weren't changing the way I thought they should. Unexpected and unwanted situations kept occurring, despite my attempts to prevent them. And I found myself engaging in the same behaviors over and over again, regardless of the fact that they were harming me. The more desperate and unsuccessful my attempts to control were, the more anxiety and fear I felt. My life was unmanageable with me at the helm. There could be only one God running the universe. Would it be Him or me? Living serenity was impossible until I stopped struggling with this question.

I needed information to help me make that decision, and so I turned to God's autobiography, the Bible. Within its pages is contained enlightening information pertaining to His character and attributes, His thoughts about life, and His purposes for people—all the information I needed to make an informed decision. If I was going to allow someone to run my life, I had better check His qualifications for the job. I was more than a little amused to realize that God's job description was found in the book called Job.

In this book, God asks Job a series of questions intended to reveal how intricate His knowledge of the universe is. He begins this inquisition with the questions: "Where were you when I laid the foundations of the earth? Tell me, if you know so much. Who determined its dimensions and stretched out the surveying line? What supports its foundations, and who laid its cornerstone as the morning stars sang together and all the angels shouted for joy?" (Job 38:4-7). He continues on for four chapters, asking questions such as: "Have you visited the storehouses of the snow or seen the storehouses of hail?" (Job 38:22). "Can you make lightning appear and cause it to strike as you direct?" (Job 38:35). "Do you know the laws of the universe? Can you use them to regulate the earth?" (Job 38:33). By the time I finished reading Job, I was convinced of two facts: God was qualified to run the universe and I was not.

Reading Scripture provided a glimpse into God's unlimited power to shape time, space, people, circumstances, and outcomes. There was no shortage of Scriptures referring to His sovereignty—more than three hundred Scriptures referred to God as "Sovereign Lord" and over three hundred more referred to Him as the "Lord Almighty." The Bible in its entirety conveyed the story of God's unlimited ability to interact in all aspects of human life. It told of God's power to create, exalt, avenge, decree, deliver, restore, redeem, reign, vindicate, protect, defend, and save. Regardless of where I turned within its pages, I was reminded of God's ability to control the things with which I struggled.

Consider, if you will, the concept of time. It is not a limitation for God whatsoever. Joshua 10:13 indicates that after Joshua prayed, the sun stopped in the middle of the sky and did not set until the Israelites defeated their enemies. While many of us wish that we could have more hours in our day, Joshua was granted just that. Time is a concept that we humans operate within and are limited by, but not God. The apostle Peter said: "But you must not forget this one thing, dear friends: A day is like a thousand years to the Lord, and a thousand years is like a day" (2 Peter 3:8).

What about circumstances? Genesis 37 tells the story of a family of jealous brothers who spitefully sold their youngest brother into slavery. Talk about a dysfunctional family! Yet God used that contemptible situation to save the Jews from starvation. In fact, Psalm 105:17 indicates that from God's perspective Joseph was "sent" to Egypt ahead of the famine; being sold as a slave was simply a means of getting him there. The idea that Joseph's trip to Egypt was ordained and not a mistake is reinforced by the fact that one of his brothers had every intention of rescuing him, but arrived too late to do so. God's plans and purposes simply cannot be precluded, no matter how desperately corrupt people or situations appear to be.

What about outcomes? Saul was zealously putting Christians to death until he had a spiritual awakening on the road to Damascus, changed his name to Paul, evangelized the Gentile world, and went on to author the majority of the New Testament epistles. How's that for results? God's purposes never go unfulfilled (Psalm 138:8).

In addition to being in control of everything, Scripture makes it clear that He is also the source of all things. Psalm 24:1 says, "The earth is the Lord's, and everything in it. The world and all its people belong to him." Ephesians 4:6 echoes this statement by saying there is only "one God and Father, who is over all and in all and living through all." From the beginning of the Old Testament to the last page of the New Testament, the message never changes: God can "grant" because He is the source of all things. James 1:17 notes that whatever is good and perfect comes to us from God above. Some of the blessings that the Bible records that He grants include salvation, knowledge, happiness, peace, joy, hope, comfort, favor, wealth, power, strength, talent, desires, willingness, and eternal life. Wow! All the things which I had been frantically striving to gain could be granted by Him.

My survey of God's *résumé* led me to believe that God was the power greater than me. Scripture had convinced me of both His ability and supremacy. As I tentatively embraced these truths, I began to experience a small measure of serenity. There remained one imperative question which required an answer before I could wholeheartedly abandon myself to His care and control: how did this sovereign God perceive me?

Deborah Galasso

"God Grant" and Me

I remember seeing a bumper sticker on a car one day that read: "God is my copilot." At the time I thought, "There goes someone who believes in God." Now, many years into applying the principles of the Serenity Prayer, I would instead have to chuckle and say, "There goes some bad theology." The Serenity Prayer has taught me that God is always the pilot, whether I think so or not. I can struggle with Him over who is going to ride shotgun, but the only thing that struggle will affect is my level of serenity.

I remember a time in my life, before recovery, when I was wrestling with God for control. Shortly after my husband and I married, the real estate market in California experienced a sudden and drastic decline. Because my husband was a real estate agent at the time, our income was seriously compromised. The bills piled up, our house went into foreclosure, and we were so broke we could not buy Christmas gifts that year.

My husband decided to help his friend, who was a construction worker, build a spec house to sell. I remember praying like crazy that God would sell that house. We needed the money badly, and I just knew this was the solution to all our problems. I prayed. I cried and prayed. I pleaded and prayed. I had everyone I know pray. Still the house did not sell.

We ultimately came through that financial crisis in a miraculous way, but it was because of God's solution, not mine. When the pastor of the church we attended found out that our house was in foreclosure, the church board voted to loan us the money, interest free, to stop the foreclosure. Within the year, we were able to get caught up and begin to pay the church back. We ended up living in that house for twenty-five more years. God was in control of the situation the whole time, but because I couldn't get my eyes off of "my solution," I missed out on an important lesson about His sovereignty and forfeited the serenity I could have experienced as I walked through it.

I am grateful that as a result of working the principle of "God grant," I'm much better at "allowing" Him to be in charge now. I am much more apt to say, "If this is happening, God must have a good reason for it." I recently had the opportunity to practice this principle once again. My pastor asked me to share about the Serenity Prayer during the morning worship service at our church. The pastor had written his sermon to coordinate with my remarks. Unfortunately, two days before the service he was hospitalized and the assistant pastor had to fill in. Being the perfectionist that I am, my first inclination was to postpone the talk because it wouldn't be coordinated the way I had envisioned. But I decided I would simply carry on and "let" God be in charge! At the end of the service, a member came to me in tears and explained how much she had needed to hear about the Serenity Prayer because of a family crisis that had occurred in her life the night before. God's timing was perfect, and this time I didn't miss the blessing.

Living serenity depends on being able to accept two important facts: God is in control and He is the source of everything I need. I can struggle with Him by attempting to assume the pilot's seat or I can willingly jump into the copilot seat, sit back, relax, and serenely enjoy the ride.

"God Grant" and You

1. What are some of the things you are trying to control in your life right now? What feelings or beliefs are preventing you from allowing God to be in charge of them? How does this affect your experience of serenity?

2. What are some things you would like God to grant to you at this point in your recovery?

3. Read Job 38:1–41:11 and Psalm 104:1-32. What is your response to these verses?

4. What other words and imagery describing God's sovereignty are found in the following Scriptures? (Psalm 9:7-8; Psalm 47:2, 8-9; Psalm 95:3; Psalm 103:19; Isaiah 6:1)

5. What do the following Scriptures reveal about the extent of God's control? Is there a particular verse you can apply to a situation you are attempting to control? (Nehemiah 13:2; Psalm 18:28; Psalm 24:1; Psalm 75:7; Proverbs 16:33; Proverbs 21:30-31; Jeremiah 32:27; Lamentations 3:37-38; Romans 4:17)

6. What do the following Scriptures reveal about God's ability to grant? Which one has particular significance regarding something you need from God? (Deuteronomy 8:18; Psalm 21:2-6; Psalm 68:6, 20, 35; Psalm 84:11; Psalm 103:2-6; Haggai 2:9; Acts 17:25; Romans 15:5; 1 Corinthians 15:57)

7. What idea from this chapter do you plan to put into practice?

Chapter Four: Me

To believe that God exists and is in control of all aspects of life is only the beginning when it comes to living serenity. Acknowledging these truths solves only a part of the serenity equation. Unless I believe that I matter to God, His power and omnipotence are simply concepts—sometimes disquieting concepts. Knowing that He is in control doesn't necessarily bring me comfort and security unless I am convinced that His power will be used in a loving and beneficent way. In order for serenity to grow, I must believe that His power and omnipotence will be used within the context of my significance to Him and His love for me.

"Am I significant to God?" is a question that has been asked by humanity down through the ages. It was the question that was on King David's mind as he stared up in awe at the grandeur of the heavens and asked: "What are mere mortals that you should think about them, human beings that you should care for them? Yet you made them only a little lower than God and crowned them with glory and honor" (Psalm 8:4-5). I remember being comforted by this Scripture when I first read it as a young girl because it reassured me that in spite of how insignificant I felt to others, I did matter to God. In light of the vastness of the universe, it can be easy for us to believe that God has much more important things with which to concern Himself. It can sometimes seem as though God is the CEO of a megacorporation, and we are just one of millions of employees working in the mailroom.

Just as distorted concepts of God can interfere with the ability to live in serenity, so too can distorted concepts of self. Unfortunately, in this broken world there are a myriad of ways that our experiences of being significant, loved people can become damaged. For some people, it was the experience of living with an untreated addiction in a family member, and the subsequent chaos and unpredictability it brought to home life, that caused the damage. For others it may have been economic conditions which left a parent overworked, tired, and too depleted to provide needed attention. The damage could have stemmed from the absence of a parent through death or divorce. It could have been associated with unhealthy family rules that demanded, "Don't talk—it doesn't matter how you feel. Just be seen and not heard." Or perhaps it resulted from depression, anxiety, or physical illness that impaired a parent's ability to nurture. These examples are not meant to blame or indict parents, but rather to serve as examples of how significant relationships early in life can affect the development of self-concept.

In my case, the lack of love and significance I felt as a result of childhood experiences became a contributing factor for the addiction and codependency with which I struggled in my adult life. I was consumed with a drive to find someone who could fulfill in me the love and significance I craved. I didn't realize then that what I was actually looking for was not so much someone to love me, but someone to complete me. God intended healthy relationships to complement, not complete one another. Expecting human relationships to fulfill in me a need that could only be met by God doomed my efforts to failure from the start. Frustration and disappointment, stemming from this futile quest, only contributed to my distorted self-concept and fueled the cycle of living for the approval of others and, in its absence, comforting myself with food and chemicals. There was no experience of serenity in this downward spiral. In recovery I have learned that the only solution for healing my distorted self-image and bringing lasting serenity to my life is to see myself the way God sees me.

Fortunately, how God feels about me is not a mystery. His thoughts toward me are recorded throughout the Bible and reveal that I am indeed significant to Him. He is the God who sees and hears me (Genesis 16:13; Psalm 34:17). While I may feel overlooked, or at times downright invisible, God never loses sight of me. I am described as "the apple of His eye" (Psalm 17:8; Zechariah 2:8 NKJV) and "his prized possession" (James 1:18). Wow! Prized possessions are the ones that are so valuable that we take out insurance policies to protect against their loss. As far as God is concerned, I am precious and can't be replaced. Regardless of the times I may have been taken for granted or treated without regard by people, God says I have immense value to Him.

One of my least favorite experiences in school was physical education class where we would endure the torture known as "choosing teams." To stand around waiting to be chosen was excruciating; to be one of the "leftovers"—the ones "chosen" by default—was humiliating. I so much preferred the system used by empathetic gym coaches where we counted "one-two, one-two" because then the choice was random and not deliberate. How wonderful it was to read that "he chose us in advance" (Ephesians 1:11). God chose me! I wasn't forced on Him because I was the only one left. He *wants* me on His team. When it comes to God, I am not a leftover and I am not an afterthought.

How I wish I would have known of this Scripture when I was a young teenager. I remember counting up the months between my parents' anniversary date and my birth and concluding that I was unplanned—an accident. Being full of teenage angst and confusion as I was, I took that revelation a step further and concluded that this meant I was unwanted. Although that was not an accurate conclusion—my parents did want me—that thought did tremendous damage to my sense of significance. What a comfort it has been to learn that the truth according to Scripture is that I mattered to God before I was even born. Psalm 139:16 says: "You saw me before I was born. Every day of my life was recorded in your book. Every moment was laid out before a single day had passed." I may have been a surprise to my parents, but not as far as God was concerned. He ordained my birth—I was not an accident. How comforting it was to realize this.

The Serenity Prayer's words, "God grant me," remind me that I am the direct object of God's actions. I am on the receiving end of all He wants to grant. The God who doesn't need anything from me because He has everything has made me the object of His affection. He wants to have a relationship with me, not because of what I can give Him or do for Him, but simply because He loves me. His desire does not depend on me or my abilities, but simply emanates from His character. God is love and so He loves, unconditionally and without ulterior motives. And that's just the kind of love I had been ineffectively seeking.

Scripture records an array of adjectives that describe God's unlimited capacity to love. His love is described as everlasting, rich, extravagant, kind, unfailing, enduring, abounding, wonderful, great, and faithful. It is a love that cannot be destroyed or diminished. It never goes away and it never runs out. It does not fade over time and it remains through bad times as well as good. It isn't simply a lifetime commitment of love; it is an eternal covenant of love (Deuteronomy 7:9). A covenant is an Old Testament term which describes an agreement so binding that in the event that one party failed to keep it, the other party was still obligated. God's love is unlike any earthly experience of love that we will ever encounter. Is it any wonder that King David said of God's love that it was "better than life" (Psalm 63:3)? Or that the apostle Paul exclaimed, "Can anything ever separate us from Christ's love?" (Romans 8:35).

It is comforting to know that my feelings of insecurity don't diminish my significance to God in the least. Despite my thoughts of "I'm not" or "I can't," He finds value in me because He sees in me what I am unable to see in myself. He sees the finished product—the person I am destined to become as I surrender to His love. Some of the greatest patriarchs of the faith shared this same struggle with self-concept. Jeremiah the Prophet saw himself as too young (Jeremiah 1:6) and Gideon viewed himself as too weak (Judges 6:15), yet God saw something entirely different. Acts 7:22 describes Moses as "powerful in both speech and action"; yet Moses saw himself as a poor speaker who was clumsy with words (Exodus 4:10). Paul wrote that he was thankful that God considered him trustworthy and had appointed him to serve (1 Timothy 1:12). When God called Paul into service, he was not evidencing faith and trust, but was earnestly persecuting the church by murdering believers instead.

But as these Scriptures indicate, God sees our potential clearly, even when we are unaware that it exists or have yet to exhibit it.

It's equally comforting to realize that our failures, flaws, and deeds of the past don't present an obstacle for God's love either. Thankfully, Scripture states that God sent Christ to die for us "while we were still sinners" (Romans 5:8). God doesn't wait for us to diagnose our problems and clean ourselves up. He doesn't mind that we are weak and sick. In fact, He sent His Son, Jesus, precisely because we were in need of a physician (Matthew 9:12). God was aware of all our character traits—the good, the bad and the ugly—and He decided to adopt us into His family anyway. What a relief to realize that in stark contrast to many of the relationships I have had in my life, I don't have to try to be worthy of His love or attention. I can simply be me.

There isn't anything more powerful or healing than the love of God. Paul called it the greatest virtue of all (1 Corinthians 13:13). There is no one who understands our need for love as well as the God who created us to be loved. In the face of hurtful experiences that have led us to mistakenly surmise that we are unlovable and defective, God grants us the opportunity for a healing relationship based on His character and grace. To those who have suffered from deprivation and neglect, He extends the offer to be satisfied and filled with good things (Psalm 107:9), while to those who have known the pain of abandonment and rejection, He promises to never leave or forsake (Hebrews 13:5). To the abused who are wounded spiritually, emotionally, and physically, He offers to bandage their wounds (Hosea 6:1), while to those acquainted with heartbreak and sorrow, He reassures that their tears haven't gone unnoticed because He's collecting them in a bottle (Psalm 56:8). He says to those whose experiences with others have left them jaded, distrustful, and with protective walls around their hearts, "I will give you a new heart... and I will put a new spirit in you" (Ezekiel 36:26).

He reassures everyone who feels disregarded and discounted that their distress distresses Him (Isaiah 63:9). And in order to demonstrate that we can count on His love to be *so* different from any that we have ever known, He went to the greatest lengths possible to restore a loving relationship with us. John 3:16 reminds us that "God loved the world so much that He gave His one and only Son…." As incomprehensible as that act might seem, God deemed it worth the price because that is how much we matter to Him.

Paul prayed that we would somehow be able to understand how wide and long and high and deep God's love truly is—in spite of the fact that it is too great to be fully understood (Ephesians 3:18-19). As we move away from simply acknowledging God's existence and sovereignty and toward understanding our significance to Him and His incomparable love for us, we cannot fail to find living serenity.

Deborah Galasso

"Me" and Me

A funny thing happened on the road to finding serenity—I found "me" as well. It seems that I had been in search of myself for most of my adult life. That search led me to many hours of counseling, multiple volumes of self-help books, and more than a few self-improvement seminars. In my early twenties, I remember attending one seminar in particular that, rather than helping me feel better about myself, left me feeling worse than ever.

We were assigned the task of making an inventory of our strengths, talents, and goals. I sat with pen in hand, becoming increasingly more concerned as I realized that I could hardly identify a few things while all around me others were writing fast and furiously. It was reminiscent of an incident that had occurred early in grade school. One day I was sent to a "more able learners" class where the assignment was to write a story about a construction site. I watched as my classmates turned in their papers and listened as the teacher read their stories aloud to the class. During this time I had managed to write only a single word: "The." I wondered why I was unable to do what the other kids had done, and that was when the question, "What's wrong with you?" first entered my mind. It was to become my inner mantra from then on.

I didn't have an answer for that question then. Being only seven years old at the time, I couldn't realize that it was not lack of intelligence, ability, or talent that was manifesting itself that day—it was anxiety. My world had recently been turned upside down when both of my parents contracted tuberculosis and had to be hospitalized for an extensive period of time. It was a season of marked change for me—new living arrangements, new school—and being sent from a classroom in which I was comfortable to a new one with people I didn't know simply made the stress incapacitating. And so began the fear, insecurity, and self-doubt which would undermine my self-concept and motivate my elusive pursuit of self-esteem for decades.

I always believed that love would be the solution for what was lacking in me, and so I looked to people to fill the void. In my pursuit of love, I constantly tried to gain the admiration, attention, and approval of others, and when I failed I became resentful as well as needy. My relationships suffered because I couldn't see that the black hole of neediness, which was swallowing me alive, left me with little love to offer others. I worried over every personal flaw, obsessed over all that I was not, and relentlessly analyzed why I wasn't getting the love I needed and deserved. I simply did not understand that human love was imperfect; I was craving a different kind of love—the unconditional kind.

By the time I began praying the Serenity Prayer, I had tried many other ways beside relationships to fill the inner emptiness—filling my closet full of clothes, stuffing my stomach full of comfort foods, and numbing my mind and emotions with chemicals. I was increasingly depleted rather than full, and I had come to the end of myself. The only way out was up. As the pursuit of knowing God took precedence in my life, I began to grasp the understanding that the only source of perfect, constant, unchanging, unconditional love was God.

A turning point in my spiritual journey came the day I asked myself why I had been basing my sense of significance on the opinions and reactions of people (including myself) rather than the actions of the King of the universe. Christ willingly laid down His life for me—there could be no greater demonstration of love than that—and yet I had been living as though I was unloved. When I began to grasp this truth, a profound sense of freedom, as well as serenity, began to permeate my life. I was free to simply be "me." I could stop trying to be lovable and instead simply focus on believing that I was significant and loved.

As I pored over Scripture and knowledge of God's love for me grew, I became less preoccupied with myself. I stopped obsessing over my flaws and instead began admitting them. Consistent attendance at recovery support groups was invaluable to the process of cultivating self-acceptance. Within the circle of my twelve-step group, I began to experience firsthand God's grace and unconditional love. As I revealed my shortcomings and the unlovable parts of myself that I had worked so hard to keep hidden,

I received the love and acceptance for which I had been searching. "What's wrong with you?" became an expression of concern rather than condemnation, and from these genuinely supportive people I learned how to treat myself with love and acceptance. As serenity replaced fear, I willingly began to look inside myself and discovered that when it came to talents and abilities, God had not overlooked me. They had been there all along—buried, not absent—just waiting to be uncovered. And I also discovered that I had a lot more to write about than just the word "the"!

God loves me with a love that is high and deep and wide. His love is high enough to reach me when I'm on top of the world, deep enough to find me when I'm stuck "in the pits," and wide enough to encompass me when I am veering offtrack. He loves me no matter what, and there isn't anything that can separate me from that fact. Through Christ, I have love; I have significance; I have serenity.

"Me" and You

1. How would you describe your self-image? How has it changed over the course of your spiritual journey?

2. How do you feel about yourself? How do your feelings about yourself affect your relationships with others?

3. Which relationships have significantly influenced your self-concept in both positive and negative ways?

4. How have you experienced God's love for you? What situations in your life has God used to demonstrate your significance to Him? How has experiencing God's love influenced your self-image?

5. What do the following Scriptures reveal about your significance to God? (Exodus 4:31; Deuteronomy 1:30-31; Psalm 27:5; Psalm 121:7-8; Psalm 139:1-6; 13-18; Isaiah 40:11; Isaiah 46:4; Isaiah 49:15-16; Zephaniah 3:17; Luke 12:6-7; 1 Corinthians 8:3; Ephesians 2:8, 19)

6. What words are used to describe God's love and commitment in the following passages? (Exodus 15:13; Deuteronomy 7:9; Psalm 100:5; Psalm 103:11-12, 17; Psalm 107:1; Daniel 9:4; Ephesians 3:17-19; John 3:1; 1 John 4:10)

7. What do the following Scriptures reveal about God's attitude toward your flaws? (Nehemiah 9:28; Psalm 69:33; Psalm 103:10, 13-14; Isaiah 42:3; Isaiah 45:5; Titus 3:3-7)

8. What do the following passages indicate about how God views your potential? (Exodus 4:10; Deuteronomy 34:10-12; Judges 6:11-16; Psalm 78:70-72; Matthew 9:9-11; Mark 3:13-19; Acts 9:1-19)

9. What do the following Scriptures reveal about your identity as a believer? (1 Corinthians 12:27; 2 Corinthians 3:3; Ephesians 1:4-6; Ephesians 5:8; 1 Thessalonians 5:5; 1 Peter 2:9)

10. What idea from this chapter do you plan to put into practice?

Chapter Five: The Serenity

Serenity is such an inherent part of my life these days that it is tempting to forget that there was a time in my life when serenity was a completely foreign concept. My life was punctuated by apprehension, not serenity. Having grown up in a home where tension and anger were the norm, I had no idea that people could actually move through life with an enduring sense of inner peace. In my world, people were reactionary and unpredictable and I learned to "walk on eggshells." The pervasive effect on me was to be nervous and fearful throughout my adult life. In spite of experiencing brief periods of calm, anxiety always seemed to be lurking just below the surface. I couldn't enjoy even the fleeting moments of peace—I was too busy waiting expectantly for the other shoe to drop.

I always admired serene people. I wanted to be like them, but had no idea how to achieve that state. One of the most tranquil people I ever met was a nurse I worked with in the psychiatric unit of a large county hospital. At times, the psychotic behavior evidenced by the patients bordered on comical—on any given day there was at least one patient who thought that he was Jesus Christ! But for the most part, it was an atmosphere filled with tension and unpredictability. Regardless of how disruptive this ward of psychotic, agitated patients became, her very presence seemed to bring a calming influence. She seldom appeared disturbed by the environment and instead used her movements, voice, and words to introduce an element of much-needed serenity. I longed to have that trait in my personality.

Being in my early twenties at the time, I was at an age where I thought that the inner peace I craved would materialize with the right relationship. I believed that if I could just find someone who really loved me, then that nagging feeling of inner unrest would evaporate. Because I was ignorant of the fact that serenity develops from the inside out rather than the outside in, my desire for serenity remained unfulfilled in spite of loving relationships. When relationships failed to bring peace, I turned to another external solution and tried altering my inner state with chemicals. Many years later, my complete and utter failure to achieve serenity through these paths would land me in my first twelve-step group where I would be introduced to the power of the Serenity Prayer.

The Serenity Prayer was not new to me. I had seen it printed on cups and posters and fancy-edged bookmarks throughout my life. Maybe it was the commercialization of it that led to me to think of it as just another catchy slogan, kind of like, "This is the first day of the rest of your life." I had never stopped to consider that perhaps the words of that simple prayer embodied profound spiritual truths that, when applied to my own life, would be life-changing.

There are many definitions which come to mind for the word *serenity*: peaceful, calm, tranquil, composed. But perhaps the most descriptive definition for serenity is "soul rest." In Matthew 11:28-29, Jesus promised His followers that by following Him they would find rest for their souls. *Psyche*, which is the Greek word used for "soul" in that passage, refers to "life, mind, soul, spirit."[18] Soul rest is the all-encompassing experience of the mind, body, emotion, and spirit at rest. People who are acquainted with this level of serenity realize that it is a deep, abiding inner stillness that does not depend on outer circumstances. That is the major difference between peace and serenity. Peace refers to the absence of conflict between two people. Because the tranquility associated with peace is dependent upon another person, it can be fleeting. But serenity, because it is an inner condition not dependent on external circumstances, is both enduring and transcendent.

People who have serenity operate from a position of calm centeredness regardless of any turmoil that might be transpiring around them. This inner calm promotes their ability to respond to circumstances, rather than simply react to them. Serene people, even in moments of anxiety or distress, continue to experience a sense of deep, inner quiet. Distress on the outside doesn't diminish or extinguish the inner experience of their serenity.

As I began searching Scripture to study the biblical basis for serenity, it was interesting to find that the word *serenity* is not found in Scripture. The Hebrew word in Scripture most closely associated with the word *serenity* is *shalom,* which can be interpreted as "peace, rest, safety, and welfare."[19] In the New Testament, the Greek word *eirene* is most closely associated with the word *serenity* and means "peace, quietness, rest."[20] While the word *serenity* may not appear in Scripture, the concept of serenity most certainly does. It is evident that God values serenity. First Peter 3:4 points out that the inner quality of "a gentle and quiet spirit" is important to God. The Bible is rich in similar passages, which indicate that God desires that we live lives characterized by serenity.

This desire was evident when God instructed Moses regarding the words the priests were to use to bless the people each day after the altar sacrifices. The blessing they were to recite was: "The Lord bless you and keep you; the Lord make His face shine on you, and be gracious to you; the Lord lift up His countenance on you, and give you peace" (Numbers 6:24-26 NASB). In the Amplified Bible the word *peace* is interpreted as "tranquility of heart and life continually." The implication is that God's intention for people has always been that they live in a state of perpetual serenity. It makes sense that if God created people in His image and He is, as Scripture often refers to Him, "the God of peace" (1 Thessalonians 5:23), then to be created in His image would imply that we were created to experience peace also.

Jesus, whom Scripture refers to as the "Prince of Peace" (Isaiah 9:6), consistently modeled serenity as He moved through His brief life on earth. He demonstrated a great capacity for being fully engaged in, and deeply moved by, the circumstances He encountered, without allowing them to affect His serenity. He operated from a position of quiet calm regardless of what was going on around Him. When there was a storm at sea, and the people around Him were overwhelmed with anxiety and despaired for their lives, He spoke words of peace which calmed creation (Mark 4:39). When on the evening of His betrayal, His drowsy disciples reacted to His arrest by swinging swords and maiming one of the guard's servants, He brought peace to the situation by healing him (Luke 22:49-51). He always responded in ways intended to bring peace and serenity rather than reacting in ways that brought chaos and distress.

Anticipating that His disciples' experience of serenity would be severely challenged by the events that were to ensue, Jesus had spent a great deal of time discussing peace with them earlier that evening. Knowing that this was to be His last conversation with His friends before His arrest, trial, and execution, it was particularly significant to Him. It was His last chance to share with them His most important parting instructions, His last chance to offer encouragement. And one of the things He found most imperative to share with them was His desire for them to have serenity. John 14:27 tells us that Jesus told them, "I am leaving you with a gift—peace of mind and heart. And the peace I give is a gift the world cannot give. So don't be troubled or afraid." In other words, "No matter what happens, My wish for you is to have the deep inner peace of serenity."

It is both moving and significant that the first words Jesus spoke to His disciples after His resurrection had to do with serenity. Just imagine what it would have been like to be one of the disciples at that time. You are full of grief because your Messiah (and sponsor!) has just been murdered and you cannot make sense of it. You are eaten up with guilt because you abandoned Him when He needed you the most. You are hiding behind locked doors because, as a close associate of His, you are wondering if you will be arrested next. Then suddenly, there is Jesus standing by you in your makeshift prison. And the first words He utters are, "Peace be with you" (John 20:19). The one person who has every right to be disappointed and angry with you is instead concerned about your serenity.

Jesus brought peace; He preached peace; He left peace; He is peace. Luke 1:79 reminds us that one of Christ's purposes in coming into our world was to "guide us to the path of peace." Serenity is a direction that our lives can take, if we to choose to take that path. Psalm 34:14 (AMP) encourages us to "seek, inquire for, and crave peace, and pursue (go after) it!" Clearly, God's desire is for us to experience serenity, but we need to do the things that will lead us toward true inner peace.

The Bible identifies the path that leads to serenity as righteousness. Proverbs 3:1-2 (AMP) says that keeping God's principles contributes to inward and outward tranquility into old age. Isaiah 32:17(NIV) extols the benefits of principled actions by saying, "The fruit of that righteousness will be peace; its effect will be quietness and confidence forever." There is a clear-cut relationship between righteousness and serenity. It is a relationship so closely aligned that Psalm 85:10 describes them as kissing cousins, saying, "Righteousness and peace have kissed!"

Righteousness does not mean that we will live perfect lives. Righteousness is the lifelong process of developing the character of Christ in our lives. We do this by choosing to apply God's principles for living to the extent that we understand them little by little, day by day, situation by situation. As we willingly engage in this process over time, we see our character change and our serenity increase. Righteousness and recovery both seek similar outcomes: character development and serenity. Choosing right actions such as those contained in the Serenity Prayer assists us to develop righteousness.

Serenity has been described as a priceless gift. Just like other gifts mentioned in Scripture, serenity is a spiritual blessing from God. Psalm 29:11 says that the Lord blesses people with peace. God wants us to have serenity—all-encompassing rest for our souls over the duration of our lives, not just a temporary vacation from stress. The Serenity Prayer is a tool that we can use to pursue inner peace because it leads us into a deeper relationship with God in which we become ready to experience His gift of serenity. Whatever disquieting moments or situations we may encounter over the course of our day, there is a principle contained within its lines that, if applied, leads us back to God, the source of our serenity, and brings rest to our souls. As we consistently practice these principles, our experience of serenity unfolds naturally in ever-increasing measure.

"The Serenity" and Me

I couldn't begin to guess how many times I've uttered the Serenity Prayer over the course of my recovery, but I am sure that if I had been given a dollar each time, I would have quite a stash of cash by now.

To say that the Serenity Prayer saved my life may seem to some people a dramatic overstatement, but not to me. My life had become increasingly darkened, not just by addiction, but by the depression and hopelessness that accompanied it. I would open my eyes in the morning and be so filled with dread at the thought of facing another day that I would become physically ill. I was no longer using chemicals because I wanted to—I was using them just to keep going. In this debilitated state, I could see no way out. It wasn't until I was introduced to the Serenity Prayer that I began to entertain the hope that I could have not just a life, but a life characterized by serenity that was authentic and not chemically induced.

In early recovery I must have quoted the prayer dozens of times a day. Trying to abstain from the chemicals that were the only form of serenity and comfort I knew at the time was difficult, to say the least. So I carried a copy of the prayer in my purse and whenever I thought I was going to go crazy, I pulled it out and begin reciting it. At the rate I was going, it didn't take but a few days of this to memorize the prayer. Each time I said it, I would feel a bit of serenity. It wouldn't last too long—I'd be quoting the prayer again a short time later—but it was a start.

Eventually, I was no longer quoting the prayer simply to stay sober. My experience of serenity had grown to the point where it became my usual state of being, and I was able to recognize the moments when it was ebbing away. Praying the prayer at those moments helped me to identify the barriers that were disrupting my serenity and realign my thoughts and actions with spiritual truths. The line about accepting the things I couldn't change reminded me to stop obsessing about situations I was powerless over and to turn them over to God instead. The line about wisdom reminded me of the familiar recovery slogan, "Think," which motivated me to ask God for help instead of reacting impulsively. I often had to remind myself that the outcome to the difficulties I was experiencing would always turn out for the best if I would choose to trust God.

Basically, all the principles necessary for living a life that was full of serenity as well as pleasing to God were contained in the prayer. As I committed myself to consistently applying them whenever my sense of serenity was disturbed, I was amazed at the results. Changes that I hadn't been able to achieve with years of therapy and volumes of self-help books began to be realized. I started to think, choose, act, and live differently. It didn't happen overnight and it required persistent effort, but eventually I had a new life characterized by serenity.

Years into my recovery, the prayer is just as vital to me today as it was when I first began to recite it. I doubt that there is a single day that goes by that I don't quote this prayer to myself at some point. In fact, just this morning I was fretting over whether or not the actors involved in a church drama I was directing would learn their lines in time. I remembered the prayer, realized I couldn't control this outcome, and asked God to "make all things right." Then I went on with my day, leaving my concerns at His doorstep. Given the depths of anxiety and depression I've come from, I value my serenity. It is my responsibility to protect it against anything that threatens to displace it. And so, in order to continue to experience serenity, I continue to quote the prayer.

I may not have been given a dollar for every time I've prayed the Serenity Prayer, but the dividends it has paid in terms of living serenity has made me one of the richest people in the world!

"The Serenity" and You

1. What is your definition of *serenity*?

2. How would you describe your inner state before recovery and the Serenity Prayer? How would you describe your inner state now?

3. What situations most often disrupt your sense of serenity?

4. Which principles contained in the Serenity Prayer can you apply to each situation?

5. What do the follow Scriptures tell you about the kind of serenity (peace) God wants you to have? (Psalm 119:165; Proverbs 16:7; Isaiah 54:10; Jeremiah 33:6; Philippians 4:7)

6. What do the follow Scriptures reveal about the conditions that lead to serenity (peace)? Which Scriptures in particular speak to your struggles? (Proverbs 14:30; Isaiah 26:3; Isaiah 32:17; Isaiah 48:18; Romans 8:6; 2 Peter 1:2)

7. What do the following Scriptures reveal about God's role in serenity (peace)? (Psalm 4:8; Psalm 29:11; Psalm 85:8; John 16:33; Romans 5:1; Galatians 5:22)

8. What idea from this chapter do you plan to put into practice?

Chapter Six: To Accept the Things I Cannot Change

In almost any twelve-step group you attend, you will hear people talking about their attempts to accept the things they cannot change. It doesn't matter whether they are struggling with drugs, alcohol, codependency, food, gambling, or sex, the topic of acceptance is guaranteed to come up. That is because accepting the things we cannot change is central to experiencing serenity. Yet for many people, the idea that there are things that cannot be changed and must instead be accepted is, in itself, difficult to accept. I know it was for me.

When I first began attending twelve-step groups and heard people talking about accepting things they could not change, I scoffed at the idea. "How could they believe that?" I wondered. After all, this was America—the place where I had heard adages such as: "You can be anything you want to be." "You can do anything you set your mind to." "If at first you don't succeed, try, try again." The meaning of these messages was clear to me—if something wasn't changing, then I must not be trying hard enough and the solution was to try harder. Anything was possible if I just applied myself.

Contrary to these messages, the reality is that there is a limit to the things that we can realistically change. If we are to have any chance of living serenity, we must understand what we can and cannot control. It doesn't matter how hard I apply myself; if something is beyond my control, I cannot change it. When we fail to appreciate this limitation, we set up a never-ending cycle of frustration and failure. As we redouble our futile efforts, we misuse our energy and ultimately become exhausted and depleted. Serenity can never come from such misguided efforts.

It is in a twelve-step group that many of us hear for the first time that we cannot control people, places, things, or situations—basically anything that exists on the outside of ourselves. There are many situations and conditions which are simply facts of our lives and cannot be altered. Consider aging as an example. I can eat nutritiously, exercise regularly, and keep my cholesterol level within a healthy range, but no matter what I do, I will continue to age. I may be able to disguise the aging process somewhat with an injection of a cosmetic agent, but under my wrinkle-free skin, the physiological processes of my body will still be in a state of ongoing physical decline. It is a fact of life that cannot be changed.

Every day we experience a number of situations which are beyond our control. We can't prevent the washer, air conditioner, or car from breaking down because mechanical things simply wear out. We can't make traffic move faster during the daily commute. Sometimes we will be stuck in long lines at the bank or market. And at other times our doctor will deliver news about our health that we wish he had not. These are just some of the facts of life with which we must live. We can get stuck in a state of indignation, bemoaning our fate, wondering why these things always happen to us, or we can admit that we are powerless over their existence and move toward a state of acceptance. One response will leave us frustrated while the other will move us toward serenity.

Many of us who have struggled with a chemical addiction have had to address the futility of failing to accept our condition. For years I couldn't come to terms with my disease. I relapsed several times because I wouldn't accept the "pickle theory" of chemical dependency which states: "Once a cucumber becomes a pickle, it can't change back." I didn't want to be a pickle; I wanted to be a cucumber! And so I returned to drugs after several periods of sobriety, trying in vain to be a "recreational" user again. It wasn't until I accepted the fact of my disease—that I could never be a cucumber again—that I could get off the relapse merry-go-round and participate in ongoing recovery and the serenity it offered.

For most of us, "the things" we cannot change which present the greatest challenge to acceptance and serenity are not things at all—they're people. In recovery we learn that we cannot control another person's thoughts, feelings, actions, beliefs, opinions, choices, decisions, attitudes, words, expectations, rules, priorities, successes, or failures. We can't change someone's mind any more than we can force them to feel a certain way. We can't "make" people listen to us or treat us a certain way. It's not up to us to "make" people understand us or approve of our actions. The bottom line is this: God "makes" people; we do not.

Until we took the time to do an honest appraisal of ourselves, most of us were in a serious state of denial about the extent to which we were attempting to change, rather than accept, others. In my case, I initially wanted to compromise rather than abandon my attempts to control others. I was willing to entertain the notion that attempting to control people probably wasn't a good thing—after all, the word *control* sounded so ugly when applied to the people I loved. I didn't want to be *that* way with them. It sounded so much better to call it "influencing," or better yet "helping." How could I think of myself as a loving wife, mother, or friend if I couldn't "help" the people I cared about become the better people I knew they could be? All these well-intentioned rationalizations were actually control issues dressed up to appear benign.

Once we are able to re-label these "helpful" behaviors as control issues, we are amazed at the extent to which they are manifested in everyday life. In fact, control issues are at the root of most interpersonal conflicts. More often than not, when we are talking about "personality conflicts" or "power struggles," we are actually referring to control issues. There are a number of ways people demonstrate controlling behaviors: needing to have the last word; giving others unsolicited advice; manipulating others through flattery or threats; as well as nagging, scolding, demanding, and complaining in general. The tendency to begin statements with "you" messages such as "You should," "You shouldn't," "You had better," or "Why don't you" is another common indication of control issues.

Although attempts to change others are widespread, they are anything but benign. Over time these attempts end up hurting not just ourselves, but others also. What we can't accept, we begin to resent. The more our endeavors to change others fail, the more frustration we experience. As we begin to resent that others are not doing things the way we think they should, our relationships start to suffer. Eventually the people we are trying to "help" see our efforts as interference and respond with resentment rather than the gratitude we expect and desire. Resentment, stemming from our lack of acceptance, begins to poison everyone involved.

Ultimately, our efforts to control and change others are destructive because they represent an attempt to play God in someone else's life. Contrary to the well-meaning and loving "spin" I like to put on these behaviors, in reality they are a disservice to the people I claim to love because they interfere with their spiritual growth as well as my own. I fail to realize that when I rush in to help, I may actually be interfering with a spiritual work God is attempting to accomplish within them. It is in the midst of struggling that people turn to God for help. When I interfere with their struggle by attempting to fix a problem for them, it displaces their motivation to look to God. Furthermore, when I attempt to change others, I am operating under a delusion of false power. Motivated solely by the desire to accomplish the highest good in an individual's life, God is qualified to enable people, and He has the power to do so. It is His job to save, rescue, and change people, not mine. It is the work of the Holy Spirit to convict and change hearts, not mine. I am guaranteed to fail whenever I attempt to do His job for Him.

The experience of serenity increases to the extent that we learn to practice acceptance. If we say that God is sovereign and ultimately in control, then the reasonable response is acceptance of life as it is and people as they are. When we attempt to change things that are not ours to change, we are, in essence, attempting to displace God from His position of authority. Accepting the things we cannot change means that we allow life to happen according to God's plans. It is the antithesis of manipulation.

While most of us would probably say that we find another person's attempts to manipulate us offensive, that is just what our efforts to control and change others are—a form of manipulation. Thomas Merton, who authored *No Man Is an Island*, said: "The beginning of...

love is the will to let those we love be perfectly themselves…not to twist them to fit our own image…."[21] The apostle James said it a little stronger: "God is in charge of deciding human destiny. Who do you think you are to meddle in the destiny of others?" (James 4:12 MSG). The bottom line is that people who have been lovingly created in God's image do not need to be remade into mine; yet that is just what I am attempting to do when I try to change them to meet my expectations.

It seems we humans have always had a need to be in control. Perhaps this is one of the many ways we reflect the image of God. Scripture contains many examples of people who failed to accept the things they could not change, and the serious consequences and lack of serenity that resulted. Genesis 16 tells the story of Abraham, Sarah, and a promised child. Both Abraham and Sarah realized that Sarah was long past the age of fertility. That was a fact they could not change. But rather than accept the situation as it was and wait for God to change it, they took matters into their own hands and attempted to achieve the promised outcome through their own efforts. In the long run, this resulted in needless pain and suffering for everyone involved. Had they accepted their circumstances, they could have waited with patient serenity for God's perfect plan.

Perhaps one of the most well-known biblical examples of manipulation versus acceptance is found in the story of David and Bathsheba. Rather than accept the consequences of his sinful, adulterous choice, David attempted to manipulate and undermine Uriah's integrity with alcohol and bribery. When his efforts failed, David used his position as king to orchestrate Uriah's demise. His actions resulted not just in heartbreak for himself and Bathsheba, but in far-reaching repercussions for the next generation of his family (2 Samuel 11; 12:1-14).

As we resolve to genuinely embrace the fact that we can't change people, places, things or circumstances, we begin to experience a sense of relief which is the beginning of serenity. It is a relief to realize that we aren't responsible for finding solutions to other people's problems. Instead of control, we can exercise wisdom in distinguishing between responsibility that belongs to us and that which belongs to others. We can begin to relax and let life happen—allowing ourselves to respond as situations unfold, rather than burning ourselves out by continually anticipating what might go wrong and attempting to prevent what might never happen.

While acceptance is the solution that brings serenity, it is seldom an easy task. Accepting the things we cannot change means that we face and admit our powerlessness on an ongoing basis—a difficult task for people created with an inherent need to control. There will be many times when I disagree with the path a person I love is taking, yet I will be powerless to change their direction. The power to change direction lies within them, not me. Acceptance means that we recognize that God has given everyone the freedom to choose their own course. When we accept another person's right to choose, it does not mean that we endorse, condone, or even agree with their choices. It simply means that we respect that God has given each one of us the freedom to choose as well as the opportunity to come to Him to find our solutions. Practicing acceptance allows us to experience serenity as we love, pray, and spiritually encourage others, trusting that God cares for their well-being even more than we do.

No one enjoys standing by and watching someone chart a course which they believe will lead to pain and sorrow. I wonder if this is how the Old Testament Prophet Jeremiah acquired his nickname of "the weeping prophet." For twenty-three years he tried to get the people of Israel to see that they were on the path to destruction, yet they simply would not listen. His efforts to get them to change, although God-inspired, were futile. Commitment to living a life of acceptance means that at times we will experience sadness and loss. We may have to let go of hopes and dreams we have for others in order to truly accept them as they are. We may have to relinquish certain outcomes that we desire for ourselves, surrendering them to God instead. We may have to amend our expectations to live with difficult situations that we never saw coming. It seems, then, that there is a bit of the grieving process involved in arriving at acceptance and we may have to experience some bargaining, anger, and depression along the way.

In the end, the difficulty will be worthwhile because there is a direct relationship between acceptance and serenity. And the more we practice accepting the people and circumstances God has placed in our lives, the more serenity we can expect to experience.

"To Accept the Things I Cannot Change" and Me

I am a person who has never cared for change. I could eat the same breakfast cereal for weeks on end and still enjoy it. I can take the same walking path through my neighborhood each day and not be bored. I lived in the same house for thirty-two years and that was just fine with me. Given this tendency, it makes no sense that I would apply myself so diligently to attempting to change people, places, things, and situations, yet I do. Learning to accept the things I cannot change is an ongoing challenge for the control freak in me.

Learning to accept my powerlessness was one of the first and most difficult lessons I learned in recovery. The initial thrill of finally being clean and sober was rapidly replaced with the realization that my life was still unmanageable. I could no longer manage my mood with chemicals, and the pain they had been masking surfaced with an ugly intensity. My life was even more of a mess than I had realized and I felt utterly out of control. So I coped the only way I knew how at the time—I blamed everyone else and set out to get them to change.

One of the most painful aspects of my life at the time was my marriage. It had deteriorated into an ongoing power struggle over who was or wasn't giving; who was or wasn't getting; who was or wasn't doing enough; who needed to change. I focused my efforts on trying to convince my husband that he was the one who needed to change. After all, I was in recovery now. I was going to meetings and learning about my issues. I was changing, and in my opinion he was not.

I tried everything I knew to get him to change. I dragged him to marital therapy. I tried to get him to read books by Henry Cloud and John Townsend. I invited him to recovery groups. Actually, I didn't "invite," I nagged. I employed a number of desperate and unsavory attempts to force him to change, including attacks on his character and threats to leave. None of these accomplished what I really desired, which was a loving and mutually respectful relationship. Looking back now, I am aware of the insanity of expecting those intimidating methods to inspire connection and love in another human being!

I was at the end of my rope. As the conflict continued and my feelings of resentment toward him mounted, I began to think that in order to maintain my sobriety, there was no other option but to leave the marriage. But because I was working on turning my will and life over to God, I paid lip service to the idea of seeking God's will by telling God I would like His permission to leave. When I opened my Bible that morning, my devotion was Ezekiel 36:26-27: "And I will give you a new heart, and I will put a new spirit in you. I will take out your stony, stubborn heart and give you a tender, responsive heart. And I will put my Spirit in you so that you will follow my decrees and be careful to obey my regulations." Although it wasn't the answer I was looking for, God had given both a promise and a solution.

The solution was for my heart and spirit to change, yet I felt powerless to change them. How could I rid myself of years of built-up misunderstanding, distrust, and hostility? While I felt powerless to change my own heart, God said that He could and would. I resolved to live on that promise and as I did, I began to practice acceptance. I stopped focusing on my husband's faults and instead refocused on trying to inventory and change my own. My twelve-step group was teaching me the importance of practicing acceptance in all areas of my life, not just with regard to the disease of addiction.

When I began to apply the principle of accepting the things I could not change, guess what? Things began to change. Within the atmosphere of acceptance, there was freedom for love to grow and hearts to heal. Acceptance allowed me to open my eyes to the things I admired and appreciated in my husband. Acceptance allowed me to see him as a person with strengths and weakness, much more like me than at odds with me. He desired what I desired, which is what we all desire: to be accepted.

Today, our marriage is stronger than ever. The power struggles have been replaced by respect for each other's differences; the sound of laughter has replaced that of voices raised in heated disagreement, and serenity has replaced hostility. Once upon a time I couldn't envision staying together; now I cannot imagine missing the sweetness of growing old together. A marriage which could have become just another sad statistic was saved because of the promise of a loving God who does have the power to change people, places, things, and circumstances.

I am by nature a controlling person. I learned it by living with it during my formative years, and I practiced and perfected it as an adult. As much as I wish it were not the case, there is a control freak born and bred in me. So with God's help, I will spend the rest of my life learning to accept the things I cannot change. It's just another fact I'm learning to accept.

"To Accept the Things I Cannot Change" and You

1. What are some situations you are attempting to control and how are you attempting to control them?

2. Who are the people in your life you have attempted to change and what methods have you employed in your attempts to change them? What effects have your efforts had?

3. Are there personality conflicts or power struggles in your life? How do these relate to the issue of control?

4. From the following list of controlling behaviors discussed in this chapter, which do you struggle with most often? (Circle Those That Apply)

- Needing to have the last word
- Giving others unsolicited advice or opinions
- Manipulating behavior such as flattery or threats
- Nagging, scolding, demanding, or complaining
- "You" messages

5. What do you fear will happen if you stop trying to change the person or situation?

6. How do your control issues hinder your spiritual growth?

7. Have you experienced the grieving process as you practice acceptance? In what ways?

8. What do the following Scriptures indicate concerning God's role in helping others versus your role in helping others? (1 Kings 8:39; Psalm 72:12-14; Psalm 109:31; Proverbs 19:19; 1 Thessalonians 5:11; 2 Timothy 2:24; Ephesians 4:29, 32; James 5:16; 1 Peter 4:8)

9. What insights regarding acceptance can you discover from the following Scriptures? (1 Samuel 15:34-35; 16:1; Ecclesiastes 5:19-20; Mark 4:20; John 6:60, 66; Acts 15:8; Romans 15:7)

10. What do the following Scriptures reveal about how God views choice? (Deuteronomy 30:19; Joshua 24:15; 1 Chronicles 21:10)

11. What idea from this chapter do you plan to put into practice?

Chapter Seven: The Courage to Change the Things I Can

Having just determined that a considerable portion of life is beyond my control, it is tempting to throw up my hands and wonder, "What *can* I do?" If I can't change people, places, and situations—the bulk of my world as I know it—then what is realistically under my control? The answer is that there is actually a great deal I can control—namely, me.

"Change the things I can" means that I focus my energy on practicing self-control. Some of the things that I can change include my choices, feelings, actions, thoughts, attitudes, beliefs, priorities, goals, expectations, perceptions, opinions, and the rules by which I live. I can decide whether I will say "yes" or "no" to the requests of other people. I have the ability to control how I will use my time. I can determine how and when I will use my talents. I can decide to ask for help when I'm overburdened or I can plug along, carrying the load alone. That's quite a list already, but there's even more.

When it comes to my relationships with people, I can decide what, when, and how I will communicate with them. My speech can be seasoned with grace and truth or peppered with hostility. I can determine my personal boundaries—what kind of behaviors I will accept from others and what kind I will not. While I can't change how someone treats me, I can decide how I will respond to their treatment. Although I can't make someone approve of me or even understand me, I can share my feelings and thoughts with them, which may influence their opinion. It is my decision whether or not I give or seek forgiveness. I have the choice to mind my own business rather than jump into the middle of someone else's problems. I can choose to forfeit the adrenalin rush of drama for the quiet repose of serenity.

When it comes to my recovery, there are numerous things that are under my control. I can change where I spend my time and with whom it is spent. I can decide how much accountability I want in my life. I can determine which meetings I will attend and how often I will attend them. I can choose to have a sponsor, and I have the option of whether or not to make a telephone call when I am struggling. I can decide to ignore or attend to conditions which make me vulnerable to relapse such as hunger, anger, loneliness, and fatigue. I can elect to read Scripture on a daily basis to improve my conscious awareness of God, or I can omit it. I can take the time to recite the Serenity Prayer during moments of frustration, or not. I am the one who decides how I will work my program of recovery.

Putting my energy into these kinds of actions is the epitome of responsible behavior and self-control. Unfortunately, I sometimes fail to change the things I can by abdicating self-responsibility to other people. One way I defer to others is by failing to express my needs and preferences, which essentially allows them to choose for me. When this becomes a pattern, I can begin to feel like a victim. By allowing others to determine the direction of my life, I make them my higher power, in essence replacing God. This is a situation which is sure to lead to spiritual death rather than the serenity I desire. I can stop volunteering to be a victim by instead exercising my responsibility to speak for myself.

Another way that I fail to change the things I can is when I am more concerned with controlling others than executing my own responsibilities. By doing this I ultimately fail the one person God has put me in charge of—I fail myself. As long as I remain focused on what I cannot change rather than what I can do in response, I will feel miserable. Serenity will be elusive until I can correct this erroneous focus.

Ironically, my best hope for influencing and changing others is to change myself. Relationships are interdependent systems that attempt to seek balance, hence the popular saying, "Opposites attract." Systems theory tells us that change in one part of a system will bring about change in another part of the system. The good news for recovering people is that because relationships are people systems, as we focus on changing and improving our selves, eventually there will be an impact on those around us. As we act differently, people respond differently. This concept may be what Peter had in mind when he talked about winning people over by our admirable behavior (1 Peter 3:1). By limiting our focus to only those things that we can realistically change, we will reap dividends in positive personal growth as well as improved interpersonal relationships.

It is interesting that the Serenity Prayer says that it requires courage to change the things we can, rather than knowledge. While knowledge is helpful and new information can motivate us to consider change, it is not action. If knowledge alone were the answer, we would all be changed by simply listening to daytime television's daily parade of experts. More often than not, when we struggle with conflict in our lives, we already know what we can and should do. What we truly need to exercise is courage, not knowledge.

It requires courage to look honestly at ourselves. If I am going to change the things I can, then I must first take a long, hard look inside, which will probably mean experiencing some pain. Inevitably I will see things that are not as I would like them to be—shortcomings, character defects, or past hurts that are either contributing to my compulsive behaviors or driving my attempts to control others. While most of us would rather not have to face these painful things, Scripture encourages us to do just that. Lamentations 3:40 says, "let us test and examine our ways" so that we can turn to God. The words "test and examine" indicate that this is to be a diligent and penetrating search. For many of us, our first attempt at this type of introspective self-awareness begins with our fourth-step inventory.

Unfortunately, it is so much easier to focus on the character flaws of other people rather than our own. This tendency was so common, yet so crippling, that Jesus chose to address it during His first public sermon, better known as the Sermon on the Mount. Matthew 7:3-

4 records Him as saying: "And why worry about a speck in your friend's eye when you have a log in your own? How can you think of saying to your friend, 'Let me help you get rid of that speck in your eye,' when you can't see past the log in your own eye?" His message was clear—we need to take care of our own character issues before we can attempt to help others with theirs. To put it in recovery terms, Jesus was reminding us to simply be concerned with cleaning up our side of the street.

We are motivated to do this when we understand the importance of reconciliation. Living in harmony with others requires the ability to promptly admit when we are wrong and take action to correct any harm that we have caused. In doing this, we demonstrate to the person involved how much the relationship matters. Interestingly enough, it is so important to God that people live peacefully with each other that His standard for reconciliation goes beyond apologies and amends. Matthew 5:23-24 indicates that if we know someone is holding something against us, we are to have the courage to approach them and seek reconciliation! If we are to change our orientation away from denying our mistakes and blaming others for our shortcomings toward embracing healthy, mature relationships, it will require humility as well as courage.

It requires courage to change the things I can because change is often uncomfortable and, at times, downright frightening. As humans, we have a tendency to want our lives to be comfortable, familiar, and predictable. Change, regardless of whether it is positive or negative, introduces an element of risk and uncertainty. For example, if I receive a promotion at work and am making more money, that's considered a positive thing, yet it brings with it a change in environment, personnel, and responsibility that can seem risky. There is an interesting phenomenon that humans sometimes experience—the ability to be both miserable and comfortable at the same time. In other words, sometimes we would rather be miserable in a situation which is bad yet familiar to us than to risk change and uncertainty. This explains why we sometimes forfeit the potential for happiness, growth, and serenity.

It requires courage to change the things I can because the changes I make will not always be met with approval from others. As I begin to honestly share my thoughts and feelings with others, I may be surprised to learn that they really don't want that level of authenticity. When I begin to say, "No, I won't do that," and set limits on my time or change how and what I do for people, my actions may introduce an element of inconvenience into their lives. They may disapprove of more than just my choices and actions—they may disapprove of me. I may be labeled inconsiderate, unloving, or worse yet, selfish. This is a fate worse than death for a people pleaser like me! It takes a great deal of courage to risk that kind of disapproval from others. Fortunately, when it comes to experiencing serenity, the approval of others is an elective, not a prerequisite.

Some of the most criticized choices we make are often the ones we make for God. Tony Dungy, the former head coach of the Indianapolis Colts, told of facing a great deal of criticism because he acted on his belief that he could coach his players according to a godly set of principles and still motivate them toward winning. The fact that his team won the super bowl under his guidance demonstrated not just the effectiveness of his leadership skills but his spiritual integrity also.[22] People unfamiliar with recovery will often misunderstand or disapprove of the principles we follow. They may wonder why we "still go to those meetings," puzzle over why we can't "have just one drink," or question why we are "using God as a crutch." People within our recovery groups may object to our naming Jesus Christ as our Higher Power. Courage will be required to respond to them honestly.

While the dictionary defines *courage* as the ability to face danger without fear,[23] I like to define the courage that leads to living serenity as the ability to feel afraid and change the things I can anyway. If I wait for the absence of fear, I may never act. If I act, there is a good chance that I may overcome my fear. Action may be just the step needed to bring courage. On the other hand, some of the worst decisions we can make are the ones that are reactions to fear. The Bible records that fear led the Pharisees to plot the murder of Christ (Mark 11:18), and fear led to a beloved disciple's betrayal as well (Mark 14:66-72). The key is to act rather than react. Action that leads to courageous choices is thoughtful, purposeful, and deliberate, while action motivated by fear is based on emotional reaction alone. The challenge for serenity seekers is to prayerfully request God's guidance before we act, rather than allow fear to drive our decisions.

The Bible makes it clear that God wants us to live a life characterized by courage and serenity, not fear of disapproval. Proverbs 29:25 says, "Fearing people is a dangerous trap, but trusting the Lord means safety." The questions which we must consider with regard to fear are found in Psalm 27:1 (NASB), which says, "The Lord is my light and my salvation; whom shall I fear? The Lord is the defense of my life; whom shall I dread?" The answer to these questions can be found in the fact that one day each of us will stand before God to give an account of our actions. Courage to make the godly choices, take the difficult stands, and change the things I can is more likely as I remember whose approval ultimately matters.

God is able to give me every bit of courage that I need to make the changes that will bring serenity to my life. Fortunately, choosing to look to Him is entirely under my control.

Deborah Galasso

"The Courage to Change the Things I Can" and Me

I have the tendency to think of courageous acts as dangerous acts. I associate courage with people like firefighters who rush into burning buildings to save people, or lifeguards who dive into dangerous riptides to rescue people. Few of us will have the opportunity to exercise that level of courage. Until I began my journey of recovery, I never considered "courage to change" as a courageous act. And while I would not equate it with the acts of firefighters and lifeguards, it is probably one of the most courageous things I will ever do.

It seems that so many of the actions I take in recovery require courage. It took courage to admit that I had a problem in the first place. I spent years cowering behind a mountain of denial and rationalization. The first step toward honesty that I took was to admit to myself that I had a problem. After doing this, it took courage to share this truth with someone else. Had I failed to do either of these, it would have been impossible to find help and I would not know the serenity I experience today.

It took courage to walk into my first twelve-step meeting. I didn't feel as though I had courage at the time. All I was aware of was a pounding in my chest and a feeling of dread as I wondered how I would be received. Would people judge and condemn me? Would they validate that I was the hopeless wretch I thought myself to be? On the contrary, as I sat in that group and listened to woman after woman honestly share their shortcomings and struggles, I found strength in their courage and a desire to have what they had.

By far the second most courageous thing I did in my recovery was to complete a written inventory of my own character defects. I say second most courageous because once it was completed I had to share it with someone, and that required even more courage than writing it did! I certainly didn't enjoy voluntarily dredging up my shameful past. I had worked so hard for such a long time to keep it under wraps. Even the requirement that the inventory be written required courage—what if someone found it?

In spite of the fact that I was discussing it with someone I deeply trusted, sharing that inventory face-to-face with another person was the single most courageous thing I have ever done. It was also the most beneficial. When I faced the wreckage of my life and the aftermath of my addictions, I understood for the first time the meaning of the Scripture: "What can man do to me?" (Hebrews 13:6 NKJV) I had faced the worst in myself and by honestly indicting myself, there was essentially nothing more with which anyone could accuse me. Because it was in writing, I could stop my obsessive ruminations of shame and guilt, and instead crystallize what was and was not my responsibility for my past. I was able to once and for all lay my past at the foot of the cross and experience the forgiveness I so greatly needed. After decades of singing about it and years of longing for it, I understood the "amazing" part of God's amazing grace for the first time in my life. The freedom and serenity I experienced as a result of His gift was both exhilarating and empowering.

Each day of my recovery, I have the opportunity to exhibit the "courage to change." There are more character defects being uncovered; more people with whom to practice godly principles; more situations which I would rather not face. The Serenity Prayer has taught me that if I am willing to focus on changing just the things I can, freedom and serenity will be the eventual outcome.

I may never have the courage to run into a burning building, but at least I have the courage to no longer run from myself.

"The Courage to Change the Things I Can" and You

1. Of the "things I can change" identified in this chapter, which do you find are the most difficult to change?

2. Are there things you need to change in your relationships, and if so, what are they?

3. Are there things you need to change with regard to your program of recovery, and if so, what are they?

4. Do you abdicate responsibility to others, and if so, how?

5. Of the things you have changed, which required the most courage?

6. Are there changes you have made which prompted the disapproval of others? Which ones?

____

____

____

____

7. What do the following Scriptures identify as things that you can control? Which are you doing? Which do you want to begin doing? (Proverbs 4:23; Ecclesiastes 7:21-22; Matthew 7:7-8, 12; Matthew 12:36-37; Matthew 18:21-22; Romans 13:7-10, 13-14; 2 Corinthians 10:4-5; Galatians 4:9; Galatians 5:7; Galatians 6:4-5; Philippians 1:27; 1 Thessalonians 4:11-12; 1 Peter 3:8-9; 1 Peter 4:7; James 1:19-20)

____

____

____

____

____

____

____

____

____

____

8. What do the following Scriptures indicate about courage? (Joshua 1:9; 1 Chronicles 28:20; Acts 4:8-13; 1 Corinthians 16:13; Philippians 1:20)

____

____

____

____

____

9. What do the following Scriptures reveal about seeking approval? (Deuteronomy 1:17; John 12:42-43; Romans 14:17-18; Galatians 1:10; 1 Thessalonians 2:4; 2 Timothy 2:15)

____

____

____

____

10. What do the following Scriptures suggest about how fear influences choices? (Genesis 18:15; 1 Samuel 15:24; 1 Samuel 18:12-15; 28-29; 1 Kings 19:1-4; Ezra 3:3; Nehemiah 2:2-8; Psalm 56:3; Matthew 1:20-23; John 9:18-23)

11. What idea from this chapter do you plan to put into practice?

Chapter Eight: And the Wisdom to Know the Difference

A very wise person once told me that "the wisdom to know the difference" was actually the most important part of the Serenity Prayer. The ability to attain serenity hinges on discerning the difference between what I can and cannot change. If I fail to exercise wisdom, it is likely that I will cause myself, as well as others, a lot of unnecessary distress and frustration. In such a state, experiencing serenity will be difficult to say the least.

The challenge that I face with regard to this part of the Serenity Prayer is that too often it is hindsight that brings wisdom. Frequently, I don't realize that I have failed "to know the difference" until it is too late. What I mean by "too late" is that I have become tense, anxious, stressed, or resentful; in other words, my sense of serenity has become disrupted. Whenever this happens the wisest course of action is to stop and ask myself whether or not I have confused something I need to accept with something I need to change, or vice versa. In all likelihood the answer to this question will be "yes," indicating that I need to change my focus. Returning to a state of serenity will depend upon correcting my misplaced efforts.

This is the reason that wisdom and discernment are necessary. Webster's dictionary defines *wisdom* as the ability to use knowledge, discernment, judgment, and discretion.[24] While wisdom and knowledge may go hand in hand, they are not one and the same. Wisdom is something that we acquire as we age, gain experience in living, and learn from the situations we confront—hence the expression "older and wiser." While knowledge is fairly easy to acquire because it involves knowing a set of facts, wisdom is much more difficult to gain because it requires experience with and response to life situations and processes which involve the passage of time. The difference between the two was summed up by Sandra Carey, who said, "Never mistake knowledge for wisdom. One helps you make a living; the other helps you make a life."[25]

In scriptural terminology, "to know the difference" refers to discernment, which is closely related to wisdom. The Amplified Bible equates the word *discern* with the words *examine, investigate, inquire into*, and *question* (1 Corinthians 2:15). This indicates that to be discerning will require time and thought. If I act impulsively, then I am probably not acting with wisdom and discernment. "To know the difference" will usually require that I thoughtfully reflect on a course of action rather than "just do something" according to my compulsive nature.

To move through life with serenity will require that I exercise wisdom and discernment as I confront the various circumstances of my life—consistently committed to examining which parts I can control and which parts I cannot. Sometimes it is fairly easy to distinguish between the two. Obviously I can't change the weather, but I can change my feelings of disappointment that we cannot go on the family picnic because it is raining. Although I cannot change the fact that there are only twenty-four hours in a day, I can change the way I manage and spend my time. I must accept the destructive toll my addiction has taken on my relationships, but I can attempt to ameliorate the damage by making amends and compensating for the harm I have caused. I cannot change my past; it is something I must accept, but I can make better choices today which may improve my future.

Distinguishing between the two becomes more challenging when it involves people. For instance, I cannot change someone's opinion of me—that exists in their mind. Unfortunately, sometimes I forget this and attempt to "change their mind" by convincing them that they are wrong. This usually produces frustration on both our parts rather than the outcome I desire, which is increased understanding. If I focused instead on what I can change, I could ask questions about how they arrived at their opinion of me, attempt to understand their opinion, and clarify my actions and motives. Additionally, I could choose to act in a responsible, kind, thoughtful, respectful manner which may favorably influence their opinion of me.

I cannot make my spouse be on time—he must manage his own time. Instead of nagging and complaining, which only serve to increase the tension between us, I can set a boundary by saying that when he is not ready by a certain time, I will drive myself. I cannot make my children study harder; they need to determine how they will apply their time and abilities. Instead of scolding them and pressuring them to change which can lead to resentment on everyone's part, I can enforce consequences if their grades fall to unacceptable levels. I cannot make employees carry out their responsibilities "my way," but I can hold them accountable for meeting the deadlines and outcomes that have been established. These are just a few examples of how "to know the difference" looks in daily life.

Anything that interferes with insight, understanding, or truth can impair our ability to exercise wisdom. There are many factors that fall into this category. One of these is what Scripture calls *ignorance*. Second Peter 3:16 indicates that ignorance involves twisting and misconstruing information, while Ephesians 4:18 (AMP) describes ignorance as a lack of knowledge and perception and labels it as "willful blindness." Those of us familiar with recovery will find the term *willful blindness* very similar to the psychological term *denial*. Denial is a defense mechanism that is employed automatically and unconsciously when we experience threatening situations. God intended denial to serve as a type of short-term psychological shield during moments of overwhelming stress. Anyone who has been informed of the unexpected death of a loved one has probably responded initially with the words "It can't be" or "I can't believe it." This initial state of disbelief gives us time to absorb the disturbing information without being completely overwhelmed and incapacitated. While healthy denial serves a useful purpose, there is a type of denial that is destructive.

It is well documented that people who live with addictive behaviors, whether it is their own addiction such as alcoholism or simply the experience of living in close proximity to someone with an untreated addiction, develop the inability to see their situation clearly. The insidious development of denial that accompanies every addiction prevents those involved from seeing the truth of their situation and taking appropriate action. As an addiction progresses, more and more denial is required on everyone's part to maintain the addictive behavior, and the defense mechanism which God intended to be a situational help becomes a debilitating way of life instead. Because denial blocks insight, truth, and understanding, it prevents us from exercising wisdom and in turn, experiencing serenity.

Those of us who are involved in a program of recovery understand the need for outside help in overcoming denial so that we can begin to exercise wisdom and discernment. Denial, like addiction, is cunning, baffling, and powerful which makes it difficult to detect, much less defeat, on our own. In order to successfully overcome denial and its effects, we need realistic, factual input from others who are familiar with the challenges we face. Proverbs 15:14 (MSG) tells us that a wise person "is always eager to take in more truth" and that is just what we find when we are willing to take advantage of the help available in a twelve-step group.

Another resource for overcoming denial and increasing wisdom is sponsorship. Although never identified as such, sponsor-type relationships are found throughout Scripture. Moses sponsored Joshua by encouraging and preparing him to lead Israel's conquest of the Promised Land (Deuteronomy 1:38). Elijah sponsored Elisha, equipping him to assume the role of Israel's leading prophet during a time of spiritual renewal (1 Kings 19:19-21; 2 Kings 2:1-15). Jesus sponsored the twelve disciples, preparing them to establish the New Testament church and communicate the message of the gospel (John 1:35-51; John 17:6-26). And Paul sponsored a young missionary named Timothy by teaching him how to administer and discharge the duties of a pastor (1 and 2 Timothy). Judging from the effective outcomes of these relationships, could it be that God considers sponsorship one of the most efficient ways to equip others with wisdom?

Proverbs 13:20 tells us that a person who walks with the wise will grow in wisdom. Having a sponsor affords us the opportunity to develop wisdom through a variety of ways. There is a type of wisdom that can only be gained from someone who has actually been where we are attempting to go—someone qualified to lead because they began at the same point at which we are starting. It has been said that "hindsight is 20/20." In a mentoring relationship, we have the benefit of learning from someone else's hindsight. Knowing that we will give an account of our actions and decisions to our sponsor can help us become more willing to exercise discernment. Perhaps the greatest benefit of sponsorship is the opportunity to receive feedback, which can be immensely helpful in overcoming denial as well as developing wisdom. Proverbs 15:32 says, "If you reject discipline, you only harm yourself; but if you listen to correction, you grow in understanding." Sponsors can give feedback that aids the development of wisdom and discernment because it is corrective and instructive, rather than critical and demoralizing.

People become willing to make changes in basically one of two ways: by acquiring knowledge or by experiencing pain. We can acquire knowledge by becoming willing to be teachable. Unless we are willing to ask for and receive information and feedback from wise, experienced people, we will be unable to benefit from their wisdom. A sponsor can serve as a sounding board in analyzing a course of action we are considering. Sometimes an action we are considering isn't wrong, but it isn't wise either. Collaborating with a trusted sponsor can help us gain wisdom through knowledge rather than relying on pain alone to be our primary teacher.

While there are many ways to acquire wisdom, the most important source is God Himself. Scripture is clear that God wants us to have wisdom. There will be times when, in spite of thoughtful consideration and helpful input, we will be unable "to know the difference." Consider the example of Abraham's nephew, Lot. Genesis 13:10-13 tells us that, when given the choice between living in the land of Canaan versus the plains of the Jordan, Lot chose the later on the basis of appearance alone. Because the plains were well watered and green, it seemed like a good choice. Unfortunately, it was located right next door to Sodom! This speaks to the importance of seeking God's wisdom whenever we are attempting to exercise discernment. Because things are not always as they seem, Proverbs 3:5-6 cautions us not to simply rely on our own understanding, but to seek God's insight also.

If we stop to inquire of God before we plow ahead in our quest "to know the difference," He will help us. James 1:5 (NASB) says, "But if any of you lacks wisdom, let him ask of God, who gives to all generously and without reproach, and it will be given to him." God doesn't expect us to have all the answers, even though we may think we should. He doesn't find fault in our asking, so there is no such thing as a stupid question where God is concerned. He wants us to be successful in this matter of living serenity, and He loves to give wisdom away. In fact, He doesn't just give it away—He gives it abundantly.

King Solomon, who authored two books of the Bible devoted to the subject of wisdom, simply could not praise the benefits of wisdom enough. He described it as sweet to the soul, more profitable than material wealth, better than strength, able to shield and preserve life, and insurance for a bright and hopeful future (Proverbs 3:14; 24:14; Ecclesiastes 9:16; 7:12). What is most remarkable about Solomon's wisdom is that it was completely God-given. As a young, inexperienced king, he requested that God gift him with wisdom so that he could distinguish between right and wrong and govern God's people effectively. God's response to Solomon's request was to provide wisdom so abundantly that he is described in Scripture as the wisest man who ever lived. Solomon's request for wisdom so delighted God that He blessed him with wealth and prestige also (1 Kings 3:9-15).

The good news for those of us who seek serenity is that because of God's generosity, we do not necessarily have to wait until we are old and gray to gain wisdom. As we prayerfully ask God to grant us the wisdom to know the difference, we can be sure that it is a request He will honor for us, just as He did for that famous wise king. And while wealth and prestige may not necessarily follow, serenity most certainly will.

"And the Wisdom to Know the Difference" and Me

As I head into my sixties, I have to admit that there isn't a whole lot I enjoy about aging. My hair is thinning, my eyes are dimming, and there are way too many wrinkles everywhere else. The one thing I am thankful for is the wisdom I now have. Yet I doubt that it has come with age alone, but rather with the practice of the Serenity Prayer.

Because it stresses the importance of wisdom, the Serenity Prayer has taught me to approach life thoughtfully and deliberately. I had always thought of myself as a fairly intelligent person. I did well in school and even obtained an advanced degree; but just as the Sandra Carey quote indicated, that helped me get a job, not live life. I didn't realize then, as I do now, that intelligence and wisdom are not one and the same. Given the impulsive, reactionary person that I was, my choices and decisions seldom evidenced wisdom. Instead, they were much more likely to reflect the quickest shortcut to emotional gratification.

It has been said that "Knowledge is power." When I began my journey of recovery, I became insatiable for knowledge. I read everything dealing with family relationships, addiction, and codependency that I could get my hands upon. I attended a variety of seminars, workshops, and retreats dealing with recovery issues. Armed with all this new information, I began to understand how I had arrived at my addiction and what was required to change direction. I felt empowered by gaining all this very useful knowledge, but I still needed wisdom.

That wisdom has come to me through my relationships with a number of wise, spiritual women. I am convinced that had I not had these one-on-one sponsorship relationships, I would not only be lacking in wisdom, but serenity as well. Paul discussed the importance of mature women passing their wisdom on to inexperienced women in an effort to teach them how to build character and live productive lives (Titus 2:3-5). In spite of my efforts to practice character-building principles, I am still inclined toward self-pity, self-deception, and denial on an ongoing basis. I need the sponsorship of spiritually-mature, recovery-savvy women to help me overcome these obstacles to the development of wisdom. As I listen to their experiences in applying the principles found in the Serenity Prayer to everyday situations, I learn wisdom from both their failures and victories. By candidly sharing my struggles, feelings, and doubts and asking for their honest feedback, I gain wisdom while practicing courage. Because they are farther along in their journey of recovery as well as their walk with God, these relationships help me to increase in not just wisdom, but faith as well.

As a result of this, I am much more likely to act with wisdom in my daily life. I recently had an experience which reflects this. Someone close to me hurt my feelings very deeply. Because I am a recovering codependent and am working on boundary and communication issues, I decided that I would write a letter to this person expressing my concerns. In order to insure that the letter was not harsh or judgmental, I read it to my sponsor. The letter clearly described my feelings and addressed past difficulties in the relationship as well. I was unsure as to whether or not I should mail the letter. While I knew that it wasn't wrong to mail it, I wasn't sure if it was wise to mail it. There was the risk that it would make things worse, not better. So I set a date to mail it, and in the meantime prayed for wisdom and discernment.

The day before I was going to mail the letter, a tragedy occurred in this person's life and it became obvious to me that it was the wrong time to mail the letter. How thankful I was that God gives us wisdom when we ask for it, and that the Serenity Prayer had taught me the importance of valuing wisdom and discernment over emotional gratification.

While aging is a certainty, becoming wiser with age is not. The only guaranteed way for me to gain wisdom is to do what King Solomon advised and pursue it.

"And the Wisdom to Know the Difference" and You

1. What are some situations you are facing that are causing you to feel frustrated or resentful? What part of each of these can you accept and what part can you change? Have you been confusing the two?

2. How has destructive denial operated in your life? What truth did it prevent you from seeing? What action did it prevent you from taking? What helped you to overcome its effects?

3. Who are your spiritual sponsors and the recovery-savvy people in your life? How have these relationships helped you develop wisdom?

4. In what ways have you become wiser? What recent decisions reflect this?

5. What do the following Scriptures reveal about ignorance? (Psalm 73:21-22; Acts 3:12-17; Ephesians 4:18; 1 Peter 1:14; 2 Peter 3:16)

6. What do the following Scriptures indicate about why wisdom is important and necessary? (Psalm 19:12; Psalm 119:125; Proverbs 2:11-12; Proverbs 3:13-18, 21-22; Proverbs 16:23; Proverbs 17:24; Proverbs 19:11; 1 Corinthians 3:19)

7. What do the following Scriptures suggest concerning how to acquire wisdom? (Psalm 119:99, 104; Proverbs 10:8; Proverbs 15:32, 33; Proverbs 16:21; Proverbs 18:15; Proverbs 19:20, 25; Jeremiah 6:16)

8. What do these Scriptures tell you about God's role in acquiring wisdom? (Genesis 41:39; Proverbs 3:5; Isaiah 33:6; Isaiah 48:17; Jeremiah 33:3; 1 Corinthians 2:13-16)

9. What idea from this chapter do you plan to put into practice?

Chapter Nine: Living One Day at a Time

Over two thousand years ago, long before the familiar recovery phrase was uttered in a twelve-step group, Jesus said, "Live one day at a time" (Matthew 6:34 TLB). How ironic that this slogan, which has assisted so many people on their journey toward living serenity, isn't a slogan at all—it is the very Word of God. Jesus chose to include this phrase during one of His first and most widely quoted sermons. During this famous discourse, Jesus discussed an array of important life topics pertaining to attitude, character, purpose, and relationships. And it was while addressing the very common human problem of worry that He uttered those words destined to become a foundational concept in recovery programs. Jesus recognized the tendency that the people in the crowd had toward worrying about material things—food, shelter, clothing—the basic needs in life. And with regard to that common human tendency, little has changed since that day. Worry continues to rob us of serenity.

For many of us in recovery, it was chronic worry that led us into our addictions in the first place. We worried that we weren't smart enough or attractive enough or talented enough. We worried that we wouldn't be accepted by others and that loneliness and rejection would always be our best friends. We worried about failure in jobs or relationships. When things were good we worried that they wouldn't stay that way, and when things were bad we worried that they would never change. And along the way, we found ways to quiet those uncomfortable feelings so we could face another worrisome day. Through food, drugs, sex, alcohol, spending, or working, we attempted to drown out the worry that was meant to be assuaged by trust in a loving God.

While worry may take a variety of forms, it is often experienced as obsessive rumination about a thought in a circular, unproductive manner. We simply cannot seem to stop thinking the worst. Worry about the past is called guilt and takes the form of "If only" thinking—"If only I hadn't made that decision..."; "If only I had stopped drinking sooner...." Worry about the future is called anxiety and takes the form of "What if?" thinking—"What if I lose my job, then what will happen?"; "What if the car breaks down and I don't have the money to fix it?" One of the best descriptions of the all-consuming nature of anxiety is found in Deuteronomy 28:65-67 (NIV): "eyes weary with longing, and a despairing heart. You will live with constant suspense, filled with dread both night and day, never sure of your life. In the morning you will say, 'If only it were evening!' and in the evening, 'If only it were morning!'—because of the terror that will fill your hearts...."

Psychologists refer to this type of thinking as *catastrophizing*. We imagine the worst-case scenario, begin to believe that it is inevitable, and experience increasing levels of distress. The effect of this kind of thinking on behavior is that it immobilizes rather than motivates. Obsessive worry and anxiety keep us in a powerless, unmanageable position. The reality is that the past cannot be undone because it has already happened. Nor can we do anything about tomorrow's possibilities—they haven't occurred yet. The only place we can productively live is in the present. Worry robs us not only of serenity but of effectiveness in living today. The more focused we are on yesterday or tomorrow, the less focused we can be on taking productive action today.

Worry consumes our time, energy, and focus. I am inclined to think that the very act of worrying tricks us into thinking we are doing something productive and prevents us from recognizing and confronting the core issue of powerlessness. It wasn't until I looked back over my life from the perspective of hindsight and many years of recovery that I could truly perceive what chronic worry had cost me. More often than not the things I worried about failed to materialize or worked out much better than I thought they would. Rather than adding to my life, worry actually impoverished it by preventing me from using my time and energy in productive, creative, and healthy activity. Ultimately I suffered a lot of needless, self-imposed misery.

Anxiety is part of the human condition and all people experience it to a greater or lesser degree. Scripture indicates that even people of great faith such as Moses, David, Solomon, Elijah, Paul, and Jesus experienced it at times. While most chronic worriers recognize on some level the futility of worry, there is a sense of "I just can't help it." And there is a certain truth to this idea. Scientists have actually uncovered a gene called the BDNF gene (brain-derived neurotrophic factor) which is linked to excessive worry.[26] The good news for those who worry is that worry is genetic—it is not your fault that you have a tendency to worry. Unfortunately, the good news is also the bad news. Because it is a part of your genetic makeup, you can't eliminate the tendency to worry. Since that's the case, it becomes imperative to find a way to accept and manage it. And that is where the idea of living one day at a time comes in.

God's prescription for overcoming worry is for people to take life one day at a time. It is exactly what He modeled for us when He created our world. Have you ever wondered why God, who is completely unlimited by time and could have spoken the entire universe into existence with a single word, choose instead to create in twenty-four hour increments (Genesis 1)? It certainly wasn't because He needed the rest! God, whom the Bible refers to as the great "I Am" (Exodus 3:14), works in the present—that is *today*.

Scripture contains many examples of God working to meet the needs of people on a twenty-four hour basis. Consider the miracle of manna. According to Exodus 16, the Israelites' need for food during their forty-year off-road adventure through the desert wilderness was provided on a daily basis in the form of manna, which covered the ground each morning. They didn't have to worry about what to eat tomorrow; they only had to do the "leg work" to gather enough food for that day. First Kings 17:2-6 indicates that at God's command ravens brought food for Elijah twice each day while he was in hiding. Later in the same chapter, we are told that God miraculously provided oil and flour for the disheartened widow of Zarephath, who was literally down to her last meal. Through God's daily replenishing of the jar of flour and jug of oil she was able to feed herself, her son, and Elijah until the protracted drought subsided (1 Kings 17:7-16). Jesus encouraged us to pray, "Give us today the food we need" (Matthew 6:11), stressing the importance of relying on God's provision on a day-by-day basis.

Lest we dismiss these examples as simply interesting Bible stories, Corrie ten Boom, the famous concentration camp survivor, told the account of having one bottle of liquid vitamins to treat her sister's chronic illness while they were imprisoned. When she would administer it to her sister, other sick prisoners in their cell block would beg her to give them a dose also. Realizing that she had only one small bottle of medicine to last an indefinite amount of time, Corrie was reluctant to share. But for many months Corrie gave a dose to each prisoner who asked and reported that the bottle never ran out until the day they were given a supply of vitamins smuggled in by a prisoner who worked in the camp hospital.[27] God's daily provision lasted until it was no longer needed.

Psalm 90:12 asks God to teach us to make the most of our time so that we may grow in wisdom. Living wisely depends upon recognizing that we have only so many days appointed to us, and when we waste one by worrying it is impossible to get it back. This must be what Jesus was getting at when He asked who could add a single hour to his life by worrying (Matthew 6:27). He understood better than anyone not just the futility of worry, but the importance of making each day count. Considering that He began His public ministry at about age thirty and died at age thirty-three, He had less than 1,100 days to accomplish the work that God had given Him. Every day mattered considerably, and He could not afford to waste a single one worrying about what He would eat or where He would sleep, even though He was essentially homeless during His ministry. He moved through this period of His life with just as much serenity and security as He had known while being cared for by His earthly parents because He was certain that His heavenly Father would provide whatever He needed—one day at a time.

Learning to live one day at a time decreases worry and anxiety because it reminds us to focus on what is happening today rather than the "ifs" of tomorrow. When I live one day at a time, I only have to handle what is on my plate today. I only have to focus my time, energy, and attention on what is necessary, required, and purposeful today. When I live in twenty-four hour increments, it makes my life much less worrisome, not to mention much more manageable. It brings clarity and focus which help me to address my priorities and goals. Additionally it prevents me from becoming exhausted and overwhelmed by overextending myself and trying to accomplish too much in a twenty-four hour period.

When attempting to overcome an addiction, I can remind myself that I only need to be abstinent from the behavior for today. When attempting to establish a new behavior which seems difficult or challenging, I can remind myself that I only need to carry it out today. When I am experiencing painful or unpleasant situations, I can remind myself that I only have to live through them today. Making a twenty-four hour commitment seems reasonable; thinking about maintaining it for the rest of my life is what overwhelms me. I can make a commitment to stay sober for twenty-four hours; thinking about being deprived of a glass of Sangria for the rest of my life seems overwhelming. I can stick to my food plan for twenty-four hours; going without a hot fudge sundae for the rest of my life? Yikes! Focusing on an unknown future is a sure way to frighten myself; focusing on twenty-four hours is manageable and brings relief. Each day I can choose to make these commitments, and as I do this one day at a time I will eventually have a lifetime of successful abstinence and healthful living.

The most convincing proof that learning to live one day at a time leads to serenity is the life of Christ. He began His ministry knowing that His ultimate destiny in this world was a cruel death on the cross. It had been predicted for ages and it was the means by which God's greatest work would be accomplished. I wonder: if you knew this fate ultimately awaited you, how serene would you be each day? I have lived a life plagued by anxiety and worry, and yet the situations I have encountered don't even come close to what He faced. In spite of knowing what lay ahead, He continued to move through this world with purpose and grace.

I am convinced that He was able do so because He was the master of living one day at a time. It wasn't just an inspiring concept He used to captivate a crowd during his inaugural sermon. It was a principle that He applied to His life. He simply did not worry about tomorrow. Instead, He focused on being about His Father's business today. The only time we see Him wrestle with the distress of the cross is right before His arrest in the garden (Mark 14:33-34). He felt overwhelming anguish that evening as His date with destiny arrived, but He did not live a lifetime of worry and anxiety by anticipating it each day.

Jesus cautioned us to be careful that our lives didn't become "weighted down" with anxiety (Luke 21:34 NASB). The heaviness of anxiety robs us of the serenity which God wants us to have. Worse yet, life's worries can completely strangle spiritual growth and maturity (Luke 8:14). Paul understood the truth of this when he advised the church at Philippi: "Don't worry about anything" (Philippians 4:6). He was well qualified to give this advice as, at the time, he was under house arrest and wearing shackles on his ankles—the Roman world's equivalent of an ankle monitoring device. Even though he was facing an uncertain legal outcome, he wasn't anxiously penning letters to his lawyer about his upcoming defense or frantically organizing a letter-writing campaign among his supporters to beseech the emperor for his release. Instead, He was focusing on gratefully petitioning God and receiving serenity that transcended human comprehension.

The truth about worry and anxiety is that they are actually a form of fear, and spiritually speaking fear is a form of not trusting God enough to believe that He will meet our needs on an ongoing basis one day at a time. Scripture clearly indicates that God does not want us to live a life characterized by fear. The admonition to "Fear not," which is God's equivalent of saying "Don't worry," appears sixty times in the Bible. We don't have to worry because God is at work in our lives every single day. He renews us each day (2 Corinthians 4:16) and gives us a clean slate of mercy (Lamentations 3:23). Every twenty-four hours is like a fresh start where God is concerned. Because He is the God who "never slumbers or sleeps" (Psalm 121:4), He is always conscious of our needs. For those of us who have lost sleep over the anxieties of life, this is really good news. God is staying up all night, but unlike us, it is not because He is tossing and turning in bed. Nor is He pacing the floor or wringing His hands, and wondering, "What can I do about this?" He sees the outcome and He knows that it will ultimately be for our good.

We weren't created for fear; we were created for life! Christ encouraged us to live one day at a time, not endure one day at a time. He gave His life so that we could experience abundant life (John 10:10), not simply white knuckle our way through it. He wants us to live above all the worries and cares of this world, but above all that, He wants us to *live*. Psalm 118:24 says: "This is the day that the Lord has made. We will rejoice and be glad in it." If God has made it, then He can see us through it. Every morning that we open our eyes, we can remind ourselves that God has given us another opportunity to *live* one day at a time. And that's something to feel serene about.

"Living One Day at a Time" and Me

I come from a long line of worriers. My mom was a worrier. Her favorite expression was "Be careful." Her mother was a chronic worrier as were both of her sisters. When it comes to the BDNF gene, it seems that I have a rich and unfortunate family heritage! And while every one of the principles contained in the Serenity Prayer has aided my recovery immensely, none has had the impact on my tendency to worry as that of the principle of living one day at a time.

From the day I began to apply this principle to my life, I experienced much-needed relief from my worry and anxiety. It was hard work at first and I must have had to remind myself a few hundred times each day to just stay focused on today. I would do that for a period of time and then my mind would unconsciously drift into the "what if" mode, and I would have to take those thoughts captive and replace them with "one day at a time." Dealing with the worry was challenging enough, but then there was the addiction. For a number of years, I hadn't been able to go through a single day without medicating myself. I couldn't conceive of not doing so for weeks or months. And so I didn't try to. With the help of my sponsor and my twelve-step groups, I decided to stop for just one day. I have now strung together over twelve years of being clean and sober for just one day…at a time.

What a relief to live one day at a time rather than anticipate one day at a time. I feel so much happier when I don't look too far down the road and instead focus on just today. Because worry is such a part of my makeup, it has required repeated practice to learn to keep my mind focused on today. I have become a firm believer in having a "to do" list which I divide into days of the week to help me stay focused. I have learned to distract myself from the "what ifs" of tomorrow by staying busy, accomplishing things today. I handle problems as they arise instead of apprehensively planning what I will do if they should materialize. If there is a problem looming on the horizon and I can take action today that will address or alleviate it, I will; otherwise I wait until it arrives, trusting that God will help me solve it when, and if, it does.

Living one day at a time does not mean that I don't plan ahead. After all, who could take a vacation on the spur of a moment? Nor does it mean that I don't consider making backup plans for situations that have a reasonably good chance of materializing. Living one day at a time does not imply living in a state of denial, procrastination, or avoidance.

While my worry has become manageable, I can still get my mind wrapped around some question mark on the horizon. But because I operate from a state of serenity as a result of practicing the Serenity Prayer, I notice these mental detours now and take steps to get my mind back on today. I no longer awaken in the morning with a pit in my stomach and a sense of dreadful anticipation. And I no longer lay in bed at night, unable to fall asleep because my mind is engaged in useless mental gymnastics. I live well and I sleep well.

I recently had a routine diagnostic test return with some questionable results which required further testing. Unfortunately, I couldn't get an appointment for the follow-up test for a couple of weeks. Many days of waiting lay ahead, and given my BDNF heritage, I knew I would be inclined to worry about the outcome. So I called my sister, who happens to be the best prayer partner on the planet. I confessed that I was struggling with this future unknown, and that I did not want to waste my time worrying between now and then. I knew that God was in control and I just wanted to be able to peacefully leave it in His hands.

For the next two weeks, I was so busy with my volunteer work and writing projects that I could hardly keep up. When my sister called to check on me, I told her that I was so busy and exhausted that I hardly had time to think about the upcoming test. She said, "Oh Deborah! What an answer to prayer. I've been asking God to give you so much to do that you wouldn't have time to think about anything but what needed to be done." I thanked her for her prayers and encouraged her to stop praying because I couldn't stand to be any more distracted!

Before I learned to practice the principle of living one day at a time, I was drowning in a pool of unrelenting worry and anxiety. Now that this principle has rescued me, I can say that I am finally living life, instead of frantically treading water. That BDNF gene will always be a part of my biology, but it is no longer dominating my life. It's been replaced by the serenity that comes from practicing the Serenity Prayer one day at a time.

"Living One Day at a Time" and You

1. How did worry contribute to the development of your addiction? How does worry disrupt your life presently?

2. What are some of the things you have worried about that turned out better than you anticipated?

3. In what ways do you catastrophize problems?

4. Estimating that you will live to age seventy-five, how many days are left? Does realizing this have any impact on how you view worry?

5. What situation that you are currently facing can you apply the twenty-four hour principle to?

6. What do the following Scriptures tell you about worry? (Ecclesiastes 11:10; Matthew 6:25-34; Luke 8:14; Luke 21:34; Philippians 4:6)

7. What do the following Scriptures reveal about what God does one day at a time? (Psalm 5:3; Psalm 23:6; Psalm 50:15; Psalm 68:19; Psalm 143:8; Isaiah 33:2; Lamentations 3:21-23; Zephaniah 3:5; 2 Corinthians 4:16)

8. What do the following Scriptures indicate that Jesus did one day at a time? (Matthew 26:55; Luke 21:37; John 5:17; John 9:4;)

9. What do the following Scriptures say that you can do one day at a time? (Psalm 5:3; Psalm 35:28; Psalm 71:8, 15, 24; Psalm 92:2; Psalm 96:2; Psalm 145:2; 1 Timothy 5:5; 2 Timothy 1:3; Hebrews 3:13)

10. What do the following Scriptures reveal about the nature of your life? (Psalm 39:4-5; Psalm 102:11; Psalm 103:15-16; Psalm 144:3-4; James 4:14)

11. What do the following Scriptures indicate about the kind of life God wants you to have? (John 4:14; John 10:10; Romans 6:4; Ephesians 6:2-3; 1 Thessalonians 4:7; James 1:20)

12. What idea from this chapter do you plan to put into practice?

Chapter Ten: Enjoying One Moment at a Time

Cesare Pavese, the famous Italian poet, once said, "We do not remember days, we remember moments."[28] The Serenity Prayer reminds us that when it comes to living serenity, moments are as important as days. Productivity and accomplishment may be the outcome of living one day at a time, but the ability to experience enjoyment is found in the moments that compose each day. If we are going to live the abundant life that God intends for us—a life overflowing with serenity, freedom, and joy—then it is important to learn to value moments.

Given that one meaning of the word *enjoy* is "to feel delight in,"[29] what the prayer is encouraging us to do is to savor each moment. Each of us can probably attest to the fact that relishing a meal is so much more satisfying than eating in a hurry. There is a world of difference between rapidly gulping your food while on the run versus sitting down to the table at mealtime and leisurely savoring every bite. Sometimes the way we approach the moments of our lives is a lot like eating on the run. We mindlessly move through them, rushing to get to the next one. By failing to attend to the present moment, we miss simple pleasures which add meaning and enjoyment to our day.

As I write this, I am remembering an example of my own failure to attend to the moment. There was a tree that grew in my backyard, and in the fall its leaves would turn a gorgeous golden color. Given that I live in Southern California surrounded mostly by palm trees, it was a spectacular and unusual sight. One day after having lived in our home for about fifteen years, I "discovered" this wonderful tree.

I was looking out the kitchen window and just happened to notice it. I was amazed—not just at the incredible beauty of its autumn leaves, but by the fact that, although it had been performing the same breathtaking ritual for years, I had never noticed it before.

In order to enjoy one moment at a time, we must first be mindful of the present moment. While this may seem like a "no-brainer" to most people, it is a challenge for many of us who are recovering from the effects of addiction. We spent a great deal of time trying to medicate ourselves out of the present moment. We did not enjoy present moments; we escaped them. Enjoyment was synonymous with the high of drinking, drugging, lusting, betting, eating, spending, rescuing, or enabling; we found little enjoyment in anything else. We lived for "the high," and the moments we thought we were enjoying were actually being consumed by the addiction.

Even when we were not deadened to the present moment by being under the influence of our chosen substance or process, we were still unable to enjoy the present moment. Our minds were absorbed with thoughts of when we could, or would, engage in the addictive behavior again. We were consumed with guilt and remorse over the consequences of our addictive behavior, or fear associated with wondering when it would be found out. One way or another, we were in our heads instead of the present moment, which is why in recovery we need to learn how to attend to and enjoy one moment at a time.

Whenever we are preoccupied with our own thoughts, it is impossible for us to attend to the richness of life that is continually taking place all around us. In essence, we are somewhere else rather than in the moment. While I am busy living in my head, life is going on all around me. This leads me to wonder how many times distraction with my own thoughts has prevented me from experiencing a moment of joy because I could not attend to the beauty of God's creation. It can be a perfect spring day, but unless I stop to notice it, what joy is there in it for me? Flowers may be vividly blooming, but only if I notice them. Birds may be cheerfully singing, but only if I hear them. It is my failure to pay attention to these moments that robs me of the opportunity to enjoy all that God has created for my pleasure.

Another barrier to enjoying one moment at a time is the tendency to focus on outcomes rather than process. An outcome orientation focuses on doing and achieving an end result, whereas a process orientation focuses on being and experiencing the journey. Any parent who has been on a cross-country road trip with children in tow understands the concept of outcome versus process. How many times during the course of the trip did you hear the question, "Are we there yet?" And your response was probably to point out interesting sights or play games along the way in an attempt to decrease boredom and increase enjoyment.

Whenever I go for my daily bike ride, I am aware of the difference between outcome and process. Some days I simply focus on the process of riding—muscles tensing and flexing; sun on my face; wind in my hair; a hawk flying overhead; clear blue skies with billowy clouds. On other days all I can seem to focus on is the outcome: How much further? How much longer? When will I make it home? One experience is pure enjoyment while the other is sheer endurance. Either way I achieve the outcome of getting my daily requirement of physical exercise, but one orientation is so much more enjoyable than the other.

Too often we cannot enjoy the present moment because we are focused on attaining a certain outcome as a prerequisite to joy—in other words the "I'll be happy when..." syndrome. We tell ourselves "When X, Y, or Z happens, I'll be able to enjoy my life." Enjoyment remains elusive as long as it resides somewhere in the distant future rather than in present moments. While we need to be both outcome- and process-oriented to live responsible and successful lives, focusing on future outcomes to the exclusion of process robs us of many moments of joy along the road to success.

Being outcome-oriented versus process-oriented is similar to the difference between being a "Martha" or a "Mary" (Luke 10:38-42). The Marthas are in a constant state of busyness—focusing on what has yet to be done—which leaves them bereft of joy, while the

Marys are serenely sitting at the feet of Jesus, being nourished by relationship with Him. Obviously the reality is that there is work to be done and we cannot simply sit around "being" all the time. But if we are serious about applying the principles of the Serenity Prayer, the more moments we can spend being in conscious contact with God, the more joy and serenity we will experience.

As recovering people, it is important for us to learn to enjoy our journey of recovery. Like restless children on a cross-country road trip, we can become relentlessly fixated on, "Are we there yet?" By focusing on all the steps we have left to work and all the character defects yet to be removed, we begin to resemble a "Martha" and fail to enjoy the changes that have already been accomplished through God's work in our lives.

Ecclesiastes 3:1-8 reminds us that there are seasons to life which include both good and bad times. The moments of life will not always be enjoyable ones. We will, from time to time, find ourselves in sorrowful or stressful circumstances. How do we reconcile this fact with the prayer's instruction to enjoy one moment at a time? Part of the key to resolving this seeming contradiction is to maintain a spiritual perspective regarding time and trouble. Moments, regardless of whether they seem good or bad, are fleeting. That is why it is especially important to relish the good moments. They are impossible to capture, and when they are gone they will simply be memories.

The same is true for bad moments. While they may feel like an eternity when we are experiencing them, they will pass and become memories also. Paul referred to them as small and temporary in light of eternity (2 Corinthians 4:17). David acknowledged their fleeting nature when he wrote, "Weeping may last through the night, but joy comes with the morning" (Psalm 30:5). When the Israelites were conquered by the Babylonians and exiled from their homeland, they were understandably devastated. God's encouragement to them was to continue to engage in life despite their terrible circumstances—to plant gardens, build houses, marry, have children, and prosper (Jeremiah 29:4-7). In other words, even during trying circumstances, they could choose to enjoy moments associated with the processes of life. They would endure captivity one day at a time, but they would enjoy life by focusing on what remained: planting, building, parenting, marrying.

It is the attitude of gratitude that helps us endure the bad times and enables us to enjoy one moment at a time. I was not too far into my recovery when, in response to my endless complaints and self-pity, my sponsor instructed me to make my first gratitude list. I have made many of these lists ever since because they reorient me to the fact that even in the worst of times, I have multiple things to be grateful for—if I choose to see them. Gratitude is the awareness of the blessings God has granted me right here, right now, in the present moment. Gratitude reminds me to focus on what I have rather than what I don't have; who I am rather than whom I am not; how far I have come rather than how far I have left to go. When I have an attitude of gratitude, I can look beyond what is wrong in my life and focus instead on what is right in my life. I can see how things could have been worse and be thankful that they were not.

The Bible encourages us to adopt an attitude of gratefulness. The words "give thanks" occur repeatedly in Scripture. Regardless of the kinds of circumstances we find ourselves in, we are challenged to remain grateful. This recommendation is found in First Thessalonians 5:18 which says, "Be thankful in all circumstances, for this is God's will for you who belong to Christ Jesus." And in Ephesians 5:20 we are told to always "give thanks for everything to God the Father." Both of these instructions were written by Paul who, as we shall see in the following chapter, suffered far more than the average person. He was able to maintain an attitude of gratitude and thankfulness because he was firmly focused on his relationship with God. It was the only thing in his life completely immune to bad circumstances.

When overwhelming circumstances enter our lives and threaten to rob us of all joy, we have only one hope for enjoying one moment at a time. That hope is to focus on the one thing that can never be removed or changed—our relationship with God. Scripture is clear that gratitude is a by-product of our relationship with God. We can be hopeful and grateful because of His work in our lives. Throughout

Scripture we are encouraged to "give thanks" to God because of His goodness, mercy, love, and kindness (1 Chronicles 16:34; Psalm 106:1; 107:1; 136:1). We can be grateful because God is our salvation and deliverer (Psalm 118:21) and has given us an inheritance in His kingdom (Colossians 1:12). We can be grateful because once upon a time we were far away from God and without hope, but the sacrifice of Christ brought us near (Ephesians 2:11-13). Regardless of how difficult circumstances in my life may become, my relationship with God remains secure and unchanged. This is an outcome I can absolutely count on, and one that brings comfort and joy the moment I choose to remember it.

Remembering that God has done for us what we could not do for ourselves cannot fail to increase our experience of gratitude. During his final instructions to the Israelites, Moses repeatedly told them, "Remember that you were slaves in the land of Egypt" (Deuteronomy 15:15; 24:18, 22; 16:12). He understood that when complacency set in, gratitude would subside. Tough times lay ahead, and it was important that they never forget the miraculous way that God had freed them. The truth for recovering people is that we were once enslaved only it was in the land of addiction, not Egypt. While we were powerless to break those chains, God freed us in a way that was every bit as miraculous as what He did for those ancients. To enjoy one moment at a time, it is important to guard against the complacency which replaces gratitude. While the desire to forget where we've come from is understandable, gratitude is served when we choose to remember.

It may be tempting to disregard this part of the Serenity Prayer because we fail to understand its true importance. The notion that enjoyment is vital to serenity may not resonate with those of us who consider recovery to be serious work and have taken to heart the slogan, "It works if you work it." Yet Scripture indicates that it has always been God's intention that we enjoy the moments of our lives. While God was engaged in the various acts of creation, the angels were shouting for joy (Job 38:7). People were created in joy, for joy. After God created Adam and Eve, He set them in a garden in a place named *Eden* (Genesis 2:8), which in Hebrew means "delight."[30] It was a delightful setting, created by God for them to enjoy. In the

Old Testament we are told that God ordained religious festivals as times for celebration and enjoyment of His provision. God was so concerned that people have the opportunity to enjoy life that army officers were instructed to send soldiers home who had not yet had time to marry their fiancées or enjoy their new homes or vineyards (Deuteronomy 20:5-7)!

The exhortation to sing to the Lord appears seventy-two times in the book of Psalms alone. The Hebrew words for *sing* include the idea of celebrating in song, shouting for joy, and rejoicing.[31] King David, who wrote the majority of the psalms, celebrated so exuberantly while the Ark of the Covenant was being brought into the city of Jerusalem that he took off his royal robes and danced in the streets. He commemorated his feelings of gratitude about that day by writing a song of praise encouraging heaven and earth to rejoice (1 Chronicles 16:1-36). David knew joy because he worshiped the God who created joy. He understood that enjoyment was found in relationship with God, not the circumstances of life. How easy it is to forget this truth by getting caught up in circumstances or, even worse, becoming complacent in our relationship with God. David's response reminds us that above all else we should *enjoy*, that is savor, our relationship with God.

Luke 17:12-19 tells the story of an encounter Jesus had with ten men suffering from leprosy. Their disease required that they isolate themselves from society and so, powerless and doomed, they could only call out to Jesus with loud voices and beg for pity and merciful intervention as He passed by them in the distance. Responding to their cries, Jesus instructed them to do as the law required when leprosy was cured, which was to go show themselves to the priest. Luke records that as they went on their way, they were all cured. I imagine the great joy there must have been as they realized that the cruel disease which had defined and impoverished their lives for so long had been drastically changed in just one moment of time. Yet in spite of this, only one of the ten was so moved with gratitude that he turned around and threw himself at Jesus' feet, thanking Him for such a miracle. I wonder how Jesus sounded as He pondered aloud why the other nine weren't expressing their gratitude for God's gracious intervention in their lives. Was He disappointed that only a mere ten percent experienced gratitude? Bewildered that so many missed the fullness of His Father's grace? Or simply resigned to humankind's natural bent toward self-centered complacency? He had to know beforehand which one of the ten would be grateful, yet He chose to heal them all. Ten men were healed physically that day, but only one—the grateful one—was healed completely.

Thank heaven that Jesus heals the ungrateful as well as the grateful. With regard to the disease of addiction, we were every bit as terminally ill and socially isolated as that group of lepers; and we were just as self-centered as any of those nine ungrateful people. Yet God intervened in our lives, set us on the road to healing, and gave us a second chance to enjoy the moments of life. May we never forget the miracle of being given the opportunity to live the remainder of our lives in serenity, gratitude, and enjoyment one moment at a time.

Deborah Galasso

"Enjoying One Moment at a Time" and Me

I can honestly say that before I started my program of recovery, I was one of the most ungrateful people on earth! I was angry and resentful most of the time, and I continually dwelt on what was not right, just, or fair in my life. I enjoyed very few moments, which is why I had to work at gratitude.

I seldom noticed the beauty of God's creation. I did not stop to admire the roses, nor was I struck by the vast array of their colors or fragrances. I did not appreciate the beauty of a sunrise or sunset. Rainbows could not be relished because I didn't like rain and gray skies to begin with. All around me was a world filled with the creative genius of the Master Artist, but I could not enjoy it because I was not paying attention to it.

In order to practice the Serenity Prayer, I needed to learn to enjoy one moment at a time. But how? I wasn't just addicted to chemicals—I was addicted to thinking. I was always in my head, obsessing about one thing or another. I couldn't notice the bronze-hued loveliness of the sunset because I was too busy wondering what a coworker meant by that snide remark. I didn't stop to admire the purple-throated hummingbird sipping from the flowers along the walkway because I was too busy thinking about staffing conflicts at work. I failed to appreciate the heady fragrance of the honeysuckle growing on the fence as I passed by, because I was pondering government waste and uncontrolled spending. I was analyzing one moment at a time and not enjoying a single one!

I began to realize that spending time in creation was a great way to get out of my head, and at the same time improve my conscious contact with God. As I began to appreciate the wonder of God's creation, I was struck with more and more gratitude for the God who did not create just a few trees or flowers or animals to appease human interests, but created thousands upon thousands of living, natural wonders—far too many to be enjoyed over the course of one lifetime. The more I began to appreciate this truth, the more I began to enjoy the moments of my life.

Since then there have been many incredible experiences that have brought enjoyment to my life. One experience I'll never forget is what I have come to call "butterfly day." On a warm spring day, I looked out the living room window and noticed a great number of butterflies in the air. When I went outside to investigate, I saw that they were migrating west and the air was so thick with them that they flew right into my outstretched arms. Filled with awe and excitement, I called my children outside to experience this extraordinary phenomenon. They were fascinated for about three minutes and then returned to their video games. But I stayed outside for as long as I could, unwilling to miss such an unusual experience. I enjoyed the butterflies that day, but it was my recovery for which I was truly grateful. Without the sobriety it brought, I would never have noticed the butterflies, let alone enjoyed those moments that became a treasured memory.

The extent to which the Serenity Prayer has changed my attitude became evident to me the other day while I was taking a walk around the neighborhood. I tripped on a section of uneven pavement and went flying forward onto the sidewalk, leaving me with abrasions on both knees and hands. Instead of thinking, "Why did that have to happen to me?" which would have been my normal resentful response in the past, I thought instead, "Thank you, Lord, that I didn't break my wrist or hip." Given my age, that could have been a reasonable outcome. I was experiencing gratitude during a moment of pain, and the realization of this made me even more grateful.

One of my favorite spots along the coast is a stretch of shore known as Dog Beach. There are few more joyful sights than dogs romping and playing with other dogs. It is dogs simply enjoying one moment at a time and being what they were created to be. And as I watch them, I can't help but wonder if that is exactly what God wants for me—to enjoy the moments He has given me and to simply be who He has created me to be.

During a visit to Nashville, my cousin took me to visit a beautiful plantation home. The grounds were completely covered in a colorful kaleidoscope of autumn leaves, and as we walked along they made a wonderful crunching sound under our feet. I was enjoying it so much that I impulsively turned to her and exclaimed, "Don't you just love the sound autumn leaves make when you step on them?"

I'm sure she thought I was crazy, but with her southern grace she chuckled and replied, "Gee, I've never really thought about it." Whereas before recovery I was oblivious to these things, now I try to notice even the smallest gifts of enjoyment that God brings to my day. I take a moment to smell a rose and I stop what I'm doing to admire a sunset or a hummingbird because these are the things that add enjoyment to the moments of my life, and I don't want to miss a single one.

I am grateful that I can say that I *used* to be one of the most ungrateful people on the earth. I try to never allow a day to pass without thanking God for the blessings He has given me—chief among these are the priceless gifts of serenity and sobriety. In light of all that He has done for me, I cannot help but feel an overwhelming sense of gratitude; to feel anything less would be an insult to His amazing grace. As a result of the Serenity Prayer, I am doing my best to insure that I arrive at the end of my life with an abundance of moments to remember with gratitude and joy.

"Enjoying One Moment at a Time" and You

1. What does the phrase "enjoying one moment at a time" mean to you?

2. What barriers prevent you from enjoying one moment at a time?

3. What are some of the things that bring enjoyment to your life?

4. Do you suffer from the "I'll be happy when..." syndrome? If so, how?

5. Do you consider yourself outcome-oriented or process-oriented and why?

6. For what are you grateful?

7. How do you relate to the story of Jesus and the ten lepers?

8. Are you enjoying your relationship with God? How?

9. What do these Scriptures reveal about why you can enjoy one moment at a time? (Psalm 16:8-11; Psalm 21:6; Psalm 31:7; Psalm 90:14; Psalm 92:4; Psalm 94:19; Psalm 119:111, 162; Psalm 126:3; Habakkuk 3:17-18; Luke 10:20-21; Romans 5:11; 1 Peter 1:8)

10. What do these Scriptures indicate about gratitude? (Psalm 106:1; Psalm 118:21; Psalm 135:3; 1 Corinthians 11:23-24; 1 Corinthians 15:57; 2 Corinthians 2:14; Colossians 1:12; 2 Timothy 3:1-2; Hebrews 12:28)

11. What idea from this chapter do you plan to put into practice?

____

____

____

____

Chapter Eleven: Accepting Hardship as a Pathway to Peace

Now we come to my least favorite part of the Serenity Prayer. Yet it is also the line I most frequently have to quote because, like most of the human race, I don't like to suffer. Not only that, the pain that accompanies hardship has the tendency to bring out the worst in me.

Each time I read this line of the prayer, I find myself wishing that it had said anything other than "hardship" being the pathway that brings serenity to my life. I wonder why it does not say "hard work" as a pathway to peace, or "service to others" as a pathway to peace. Those ideas seem logical to me. But suffering? It does not make sense to my very comfort-oriented self that suffering could bring peace, because the two appear to be so opposed to each other. From my point of view, suffering is associated with pain while peace, that is serenity, implies comfort. Unfortunately, this is not what Scripture teaches. If I am to attain the serenity I so desire, it is important to reevaluate the concepts of hardship and suffering, as well as their relationship to serenity.

It is easy to delude ourselves into believing that once we give up our addictive, compulsive behaviors and instead commit ourselves to the diligent practice of recovery principles, suffering will be a thing of the past. After all, as we travel the road to recovery it becomes obvious that much of our suffering was self-induced. It seems logical that if we just stop doing those things that brought us pain we will be free of suffering. This mistaken belief that our lives can, and should, be free of hardship is not just confined to those of us who are in recovery. Many Christians fall into the trap of believing that, having committed their life to Christ, it will be smooth sailing from then on. The author of the Serenity Prayer stressed that "Christianity was not protection against misfortune, but a basic trust that put misfortune in perspective."[32] Christ said that in this life we *will* have tribulation, not that we *might* have tribulation (John 16:33 KJV). The Greek word *thlipsis,* used for tribulation, can mean pressure, anguish, persecution, and trouble.[33] Hardship is a certainty in this life; we will all experience it at one time or another, in one form or another, regardless of how spiritually connected we are.

When it comes to suffering, the playing field is level and no one is exempt—not even Jesus Christ, the Son of God. Scripture reveals that He experienced hardship throughout His brief life on earth. He was a homeless, itinerate preacher under constant public criticism whose life was endangered by those seeking to kill Him. His hardships ultimately culminated in the worst kind of suffering—death on a cross (Luke 23:32-33). Yet God used this suffering and death to accomplish His greatest coup over evil—the redemption of the entire human race. The apostle Peter suffered persecution in the form of flogging and more than one imprisonment simply for starting a new "religion" (Acts 5:18, 40), not to mention the emotional suffering he experienced as a result of betraying Christ.

And then there is the biblical poster child for suffering—the apostle Paul. By his own account he was imprisoned frequently, flogged five times—which resulted in receiving one hundred and ninety-five lashes altogether—beaten with rods three times, shipwrecked three times, as well as endangered and on the run from robbers, Jews, Gentiles, and false Christians (2 Corinthians 11:23-28). As if this were not enough, Acts 14:19 indicates that one time he was stoned and left for dead! In spite of this extensive array of hardships, he authored an epistle, Philippians, devoted to the theme of joy and written during one of his many imprisonments. Wow! It makes me exhausted when I read this list, and more than a little embarrassed at my bouts with self-pity, considering how little I have suffered in my life by comparison. There are a multitude of others who could be mentioned here whose suffering accomplished great things for the kingdom of God. They were able to do so because they understood that hardship and suffering, in the hands of a loving God, were actually intended for good rather than harm.

As I survey Scripture, it becomes apparent that suffering is God's tool for developing maturity in people. I wonder how many times I have petitioned God to help me become a better person, unaware that what I was actually praying for was hardship because that is the process God uses to stimulate growth. God is concerned with developing my character, not my comfort. He warns us away from pursuing what is known in recovery circles as "the easier, softer way." Matthew 7:14 explains that the road that leads to life is narrow, therefore more difficult, and few people find it. Perhaps the reason why so few find it is because they are too busy enjoying the relative comfort and ease of the broad road.

God's formula for developing character is found in Romans 5:3-4 (NASB) which says: "but we also exult in our tribulations, knowing that tribulation brings about perseverance; and perseverance, proven character; and proven character, hope." This spiritual principle is repeated in James 1:3-4 which reminds us that "testing," that is hardship, develops perseverance and perseverance develops maturity and wholeness. If I want my character defects to be replaced with wholeness, endurance, and hope, then I must accept hardship as part of the process.

Too often I am guilty of wanting God to use some other tool for character development rather than the tool of suffering. Yet the reality is that the methods that Scripture associates with spiritual development are often sharp and/or painful. Jesus talked about being pruned (John 15:2); Paul talked about pressing on (Philippians 3:12); the writer of Hebrews talked about being spurred on (Hebrews 10:24 NIV); and Peter discussed being refined by fire (1 Peter 1:7). Ouch! Too often I long for a magician god whose tool is a magic wand, rather than a craftsman God who uses a chisel. The magician god simply waves his magic wand and "poof"—I'm changed. The craftsman God chips away little by little, and it hurts. One kind of god creates an illusion that has no substance, but the true God creates a genuine masterpiece which endures into the ages.

Hosea 5:15 indicates that misery motivates us to diligently seek God. Hardship is the pathway to peace and serenity because it keeps me relying on God. As much as I hate to admit this, when my life is comfortable and easy I tend to go on a spiritual vacation. I am not inclined to pray or read my Bible with as much consistency. I fail to be on guard against my spiritual enemy. My perspective begins to change, and I am much more likely to focus on me and my comfort rather than God and His will. I begin to forget that it is about Him, not me. I become self-centered once again. Hardship leads to serenity because it helps me refocus my attention. The idea that hardship ultimately leads us back to God was reinforced by Peter who pointed out that one of the purposes of suffering is to wean us from selfishness and refocus us on pursuing the will of God (1 Peter 4:1-2).

Hardship is a pathway to peace and serenity because it so clearly reminds me of my limitations and powerlessness. Unfortunately in my case, desperation is often a prerequisite to admitting my powerlessness. When I find myself in impossible situations, I am forced to my knees and must once again acknowledge that there is a power greater than myself. It is not until I come to the end of myself that I am able to look to God, the true source of power. Scripture contains many, many examples of God's intervention in situations which, from a human perspective, appeared desperate and impossible: Moses and the Israelites hemmed in with the Jordan River on one side and the entire Egyptian army on the other (Exodus 14:9-31); Gideon's squadron of three hundred men equipped with torches and pitchers fighting legions of Midianites (Judges 7:1-25); a teenage shepherd boy armed with a simple slingshot taking on a fully armed giant (1 Samuel 17:20-51); Daniel thrown into a den of hungry lions impatiently waiting for dinner (Daniel 6:16-23). Each of these impossible situations found successful resolution through God's unlimited power.

Hardship forces me to admit that I am truly powerless, but God is not. In describing the impact hardship had on his life, Paul said: "We were under great pressure, far beyond our ability to endure, so that we despaired of life itself. Indeed, we felt we had received the sentence of death. But this happened that we might not rely on ourselves but on God, who raises the dead" (2 Corinthians 1:8-9 NIV). He went on to say that he was convinced that God would continue to deliver him. When we experience God's intervention in desperate situations, it becomes an anchor point of hope in our lives. These anchor points can help us when we face future situations which test the limits of our power, ability, and endurance. Our resilience to adversity is built, and we are able to face hardship with serenity by remembering that, with God's help, we have come through difficulties in the past and will continue to do so in the future.

The pathway of hardship ultimately leads to serenity because it puts God's love, faithfulness, and power on display in our lives. It is only when we are in situations that are beyond our control that we can learn firsthand that He does for us what we cannot do for ourselves. Psalm 34:6 says that God saves us out of all our troubles. Hardship ultimately results in praise, awe, and a deeper faith in God as He rescues us. If there were no such thing as hardship, deepening faith in Him and joy in His acts of salvation would be impossible to appreciate.

Unfortunately, when I am in the middle of a painful situation which persists, it is tempting to mistakenly believe that God is displeased with me or, worse yet, has somehow abandoned me. That is why Peter advised us to avoid being "surprised at the fiery trials" (1 Peter 4:12-13). Suffering does not necessarily mean that I have drifted out of His will. On the contrary, Second Timothy 3:12 says that "everyone who wants to live a godly life in Christ Jesus will suffer persecution." The Bible makes it clear that, in the life of a believer, hardship is a form of God's discipline rather than His judgment, and that He disciplines "those he loves" (Hebrews 12:6). The passage goes on to say, "No discipline is enjoyable while it is happening—it is painful! But afterward there will be a peaceful harvest of right living for those who are trained in this way" (Hebrews 12:11). So the big question is: will I let myself be trained by it? The choice is mine alone.

Consequently, the issue for serenity seekers is not *if* we suffer; the issue is *how* we suffer. This leads us to the idea of attitude. The Serenity Prayer says "*accepting* hardship." There is that "A" word again! To *accept* means "to receive something offered with a consenting mind."[34] It is much different than to *tolerate,* which means "to put up with."[35] Therein lies one of my biggest obstacles to serenity. Too often I simply put up with hardship rather than receive it willingly. I complain about it to anyone who will listen. I wonder, "Why me?" and throw myself a pity party. My resentment at the injustice of my suffering spills over into my relationships with others. These attempts to fight hardship, rather than willingly receive it, result in my becoming sicker rather than more serene. Without the right attitude toward hardship, I run the risk of attempting to avoid hardship altogether by relapsing into compulsive behaviors as a way to numb myself from the pain. Unfortunately, the only surefire way to not feel pain is to be dead, and so I may resort to trying to "deaden" myself. In such a state, there can be no experience of serenity. It is not until I stop fighting hardship and receive it willingly instead that I can benefit from it.

Scripture is clear that God intends for hardship to serve a useful purpose. While on the surface the persecution of the first Jewish Christians in Jerusalem appeared to be a terrible injustice, it was just that persecution which dispersed the new believers into other parts of the world, thereby spreading the gospel (Acts 11:19-21). Had there been no persecution of the early church, the gospel would have spread, no doubt, but at a much slower pace. It becomes easier to accept hardship willingly when I remember that hardship can produce far-reaching, profitable results that I may not be able to anticipate at the time.

Successful coaches understand the importance of training athletes not simply to perform well, but to handle hardship also. Because of the many things that can go wrong during a sporting event, wise coaches attempt to prepare their athletes to meet these possibilities. The methods that they use to accomplish this are varied, and at times drastic. Equipment may be purposely sabotaged in order to teach a swimmer that she can swim fast even though her goggles are filling with water. Distractions may be created by throwing pillows at a quarterback in order to prepare him to stand in the pocket and pass while a three-hundred-pound linebacker is closing in. An inaccurate call may be intentionally made during practice in order to teach the athlete to retain her composure with officials during game time controversies. And conditions such as fatigue and hunger may be allowed to simulate jet lag conditions which accompany long-distance travel. Because these situations are likely to happen, exposure to hardship is intended to prepare rather than punish. Hardship leads to serenity because it equips us to cope with adversity that lies ahead, which due to our inexperience we may not foresee. Just like a wise coach, God uses hardship to prepare us for what He knows we will encounter in the future.

Hardship not only assists in the development of character, it reveals it also. God uses hardship as a way of exposing what is in our hearts (Deuteronomy 8:2). When the heat is turned up, character—as well as character defects—is revealed. It is not so difficult to evidence love, patience, and kindness when everything is going smoothly, but what about when the pressure is on? What made the suffering of Christ so remarkable was not that He suffered, but rather the way He suffered. Scripture identifies Him as the model for suffering because the character He evidenced under inordinate pressure was the same godly character He had evidenced over the course of His ministry. Throughout the ordeal of His arrest, sentencing, and death, we see Him showing not just acceptance of His circumstances, but love, patient restraint, forgiveness, and acts of kindness as well. He healed the ear of the high priest's servant during His arrest in the garden (Luke 22:50-51); expressed concern for the destiny of the weeping women as He stumbled, half dead, down the road to His execution (Luke 23:27-31); and offered forgiveness to His executioners as well as the doomed convicts at His sides (Luke 23:34, 42-43).

Hardship can be a tool for growth because it brings me face to face with the character I truly have versus the character I imagine I have. In spite of my conscious attempts to practice self-awareness, the truth is that I often don't know my character makeup as well as I think I do. I am a lot like Peter who, during the comfort and safety of the Passover dinner, believed that he had the depth of character necessary to die for Christ, yet during a time of testing a few hours later denied even knowing Him three times (Mark 14:37; John 18:17, 25, 27).

While hardship can reveal character defects that still need to be removed, it can also reveal character growth that the Holy Spirit has developed within me. Sometimes my response to hardship reveals positive changes in my character that I would not otherwise notice. It may be while I am under pressure that I begin to realize that my first response is to turn to God in prayer, rather than run away; or to head to the telephone to call my sponsor rather than to the refrigerator; or to calmly express my feelings rather than lash out in anger. Understanding that hardship plays a positive role in maturity and character development can motivate me to refrain from codependent behavior as well. If God uses hardship to reveal areas of both growth and need for growth in my life, He can do the same for others if I don't attempt to circumvent the process by rescuing them from their difficulties.

Hardship can be instrumental in helping me to develop empathy. Another meaning attached to the Greek word for *tribulation* is "burden."[36] As I willingly allow myself to be trained by hardship, I develop sensitivity to the suffering of others as well as the ability and inclination to do what Scripture advises and help them carry their burden. Having walked through pain and suffering, I am equipped to offer comfort to others in a supportive, helpful manner. The opportunity to learn to put hardship into perspective is one of the most valuable aspects of involvement in a twelve-step group. As experiences with hardship are mutually shared, I am reminded that I am not alone in my suffering. Other people suffer as well, often to an even greater degree. I am helped to resist the tendency to exaggerate my own hardship. It is only as I put my suffering in its proper perspective that I gain the ability to benefit from it versus simply endure it.

People's responses to suffering basically fall into two categories: some people become better through hardship, while others become bitter. All of us have probably had experiences with both of these groups. The people who become better as a result of their hardships inspire and motivate us, while those who become bitter make us want to flee from their negativity and resentment. Spiritually speaking, better or bitter translates into hardship having the potential to make us either soft and pliable or hard and brittle. In a soft and pliable state we are ready to be gently molded by the hands of God into someone suitable for a purpose in His kingdom. On the other hand, a hard, brittle state limits our usefulness and forces Him to go back to work with the chisel, rather than the tender touch of His hands.

It is the attitude of willingness that will determine which potential is realized. And fortunately for us and our quest for living serenity, willingness is a choice.

"Accepting Hardship as a Pathway to Peace" and Me

As much as I complain about suffering, the truth is I haven't really suffered much. Unfortunately, that does not stop me from the tendency to exaggerate my own minor hardships. As I look at the lives of other people, I realize that it is not difficult to find someone else who has suffered far more than I have. In light of this, the hardship that I have learned the most from is not one that I experienced, but one that was experienced by someone I love. Because God gave me the opportunity to walk alongside this person during their time of suffering, I was given the chance to learn a great deal about how God can use suffering to promote health, healing, and serenity.

My sister was the primary caregiver for our mother, who had been slowly degenerating from the effects of early-onset Alzheimer's for a number of years. The activities necessitated by her care took a terrible toll on my sister's lower back, and eventually she ruptured a disc which required surgery. Our mother was placed in a nursing home, and my sister was placed on bed rest for several weeks while she awaited her surgery date. "Bed rest" was actually a misnomer as my sister was in extreme pain, barely able to walk to the bathroom and almost completely unable to care for herself.

I will never forget the day I arrived to check on her status. I found her in bed curled up in a fetal position, crying and writhing in debilitating pain. Never in my life had I seen my sister in such a helpless, powerless state. I was a nurse and used to seeing people in pain, yet I felt completely powerless to know how to help her deal with the weeks of pain that must be endured until her surgery date. I left her bedroom and went into the living room where I silently cried and called upon God to intervene. My sister called me back into her bedroom, and although she was not practicing her faith at that point in her life, she asked me to lay hands on her and pray for her pain, which I did.

I cannot remember what I said in that prayer, but I am sure that I acknowledged God's power to intervene in her pain in the face of our powerlessness. After that prayer, she began to feel better. Although she had never had a history of medication addiction, she had not been taking the pain medication that her doctor had prescribed because she feared becoming addicted. Because she trusted my medical experience, I was able to help her understand the benefits of taking it as prescribed on a temporary basis. She hadn't been eating because she was in too much pain to walk to the kitchen, so I began cooking meals for her so that she could nourish her body. Because she was flat on her back with lots of time to fill, I encouraged her to begin reading the Bible I had given her years before so that her soul could be nourished as well.

By the day of surgery, she was actually able to walk. After the operation, as the surgeon described the extent of the damage to her spine, he marveled that she had been able to walk at all. After release from the hospital, a long course of rehabilitation followed. We were excited at how God had brought her through this time of hardship, but in reality the trial was far from over. When God brings hardship into our life, it is always to accomplish a purpose within us. There were still more issues that God wanted to reveal to my sister.

While she was recovering from surgery, the company that she worked for notified her that they would not hold her job open for her. As a result of this, she was put into a terrible financial bind and was unable to pay her mortgage. As the debt mounted, she began to see that the unmanageability of her finances had started long before she lost her job. She had been compulsively using credit cards for years and, until she lost her job, had managed to precariously juggle them by robbing Peter to pay Paul, so to speak. As her denial subsided and she saw the true condition of both her finances and her life, she became able to admit her powerlessness and reach out to God in humility and true repentance.

Had it not been for the hardship and suffering she experienced, I do not think that her denial would have subsided. Because I had been in recovery for a number of years, I had tried on several occasions to talk to her about her life, only to have her casually dismiss my concerns. The only thing drastic enough to get her attention was the aftermath of a back injury. Desperation in the face of an impossible situation led to willingness, willingness led to admitting her powerlessness, and admitting her powerlessness led to confessing her need for God. As of the time of this writing, my sister has not used a credit card in over five years. She relies completely on God, not credit, and all of her material needs have been met one day at a time. She looks back at her season of hardship with gratitude because of the rich, rewarding relationship she now enjoys with God.

One of the best things to have resulted from this experience of hardship is the relationship that my sister and I now share. We were born to be sisters, but hardship has made us best friends. Sharing in her burden forged a bond between the two of us that is sweet, deep, and enduring. Walking through this impossible situation together has deepened our faith in God in a way that years of Sunday sermons could not.

I doubt that I am ever going to embrace hardship. I think my inclination will always be toward wanting change, growth, and serenity to come an easier, softer way. And while I have not yet learned to consider hardship my friend, I owe one of the deepest, most rewarding friendships of my life to it.

"Accepting Hardship as a Pathway to Peace" and You

1. What is your typical attitude toward hardship and suffering?

____

____

2. How do you attempt to escape hardship?

____

____

3. How has God used hardship to accomplish health and healing in your life?

____

____

4. What impossible situations has God rescued you from?

____

____

____

____

5. Do you believe you are allowing yourself to be trained by hardship? How?

____

____

____

____

6. Do you tend to willingly receive hardship, or do you tend to put up with it?

____

____

7. How has hardship revealed character strengths which you were not aware you possessed?

____

____

8. What character defects has suffering revealed?

9. What hardship in your life has helped you to develop empathy?

10. Would you describe your overall response to hardship as better or bitter? Why?

11. What do the following Scriptures disclose concerning Christ's hardships? (Isaiah 53:3; Matthew 8:20; Mark 8:31; Luke 24:46-47; Hebrews 2:9-10; Hebrews 5:8; Hebrews 13:12; 1 Peter 2:21-23)

12. What do the following Scriptures indicate about the purposes and results of hardship? (1 Chronicles 29:17; Psalm 119:71; Jeremiah 9:7; Luke 14:27; Romans 8:17; 2 Corinthians 4:17-18; Philippians 1:29; Philippians 3:10; 2 Thessalonians 1:4; Hebrews 12:7; James 1:12; James 5:10-11; 1 Peter 2:19-20; 1 Peter 4:1, 13, 16)

12. What do the following Scriptures tell you about God's response to your hardship? (Exodus 3:7-8; Job 36:15; Psalm 10:14; Psalm 22:24; Psalm 34:18; Psalm 46:1; Psalm 119:50; 2 Corinthians 7:5-6; Revelation 2:2-3)

13. What do the following Scriptures reveal about character and maturity? (Luke 6:43-45; Luke 8:14; Ephesians 4:13-15; James 1:2-4)

14. What do the following Scriptures suggest about the relationship between hardship and empathy? (2 Timothy 2:3; Hebrews 2:18; Hebrews 13:3)

15. What idea from this chapter do you plan to put into practice?

Chapter Twelve: Taking as Jesus Did

I always associate Jesus with giving, not taking. After all, He gave His life, and what more could someone give than that? But before He gave so much, He took so much. As I reflect upon this phrase in the prayer, I wonder: how did Jesus "take" the world and what can I learn about living serenity from His example? Fortunately for those of us seeking serenity, we do not have to guess at the answers; the four Gospels of the New Testament leave us a revealing picture of the manner in which He approached life.

Jesus "took" the world with clear priorities. He understood the meaning of the familiar recovery slogan, "First things first." In everything that He said and did, it was clear that God was the number one priority in His life. When asked to select one commandment as the greatest, He chose: "...love the Lord your God with all your heart, all your soul, and all your mind" (Matthew 22:37). Relationship with God was to be an all-consuming, whole-person experience, not just a religious concept. He understood that "God first" was an either/or statement.

During His ministry, Jesus encountered many people unable to make a commitment to God because their priorities were somewhere else: the rich young man who was concerned with his finances (Mark 10:17-23); the disciple who needed to bury his father (Matthew 8:21-22); the man who needed to attend to affairs at home (Luke 9:61-62). While on the surface these explanations seemed reasonable, Jesus realized that they were actually forms of rationalization. He knew that it was easy for people to find all kinds of plausible excuses for failure to give God the number one position in their life. He often challenged people's priorities because He knew that if God were given highest priority, everything else in life would fall into place.

During His first public sermon, Jesus challenged the crowd to stop focusing on material needs and instead make God their primary concern (Matthew 6:33). Jesus recognized that the very human tendency toward attaching ourselves to material things in an effort to feel secure actually squeezes the God of peace and serenity out of our lives. It is remarkable that nowhere in the Gospels do we see Jesus concerning Himself with "things." He understood that God was the source of both life and good gifts (Matthew 7:9-11), and so He concerned Himself with God and allowed God to take care of "things." He was so sure that all resources were God's resources that He didn't even find it necessary to pack a lunch prior to His evangelistic excursions. Yet it is recorded on at least two occasions that God fed not only Him, but thousands of others as well (Mark 6:30-44; Mark 8:1-9). He understood that because God was the source of all things, God's economy was far different than the world's economy, and things were never how they appeared by the world's standards. In God's economy, the least are greatest; the weak are strong; a little becomes much; the impossible is possible; the last become first; the rejected are chosen; the humble are exalted; the givers are more blessed than the takers; and death leads to new life.

Because relationship with God was the highest priority in His life, Jesus "took" the world with a lot of prayer. He recognized that prayer was the tool for improving and maintaining His awareness of God and His will. Whether it meant rising before the light of day (Mark 1:35) or going off to the wilderness (Luke 5:16), He found a way to carve time out of His busy, purpose-driven day for prayer. He never made an important decision without prayer, and Scripture indicates that He prayed prior to choosing the twelve disciples (Luke 6:12-13), before He resurrected Lazarus (John 11:41-42), and while He struggled with the prospect of the cross (Matthew 26:36-45). His example reminds us that prayer and meditation are important vehicles for improving our conscious contact with God and keeping Him at the center of our lives.

Jesus "took" the world with a clear sense of identity and purpose. He knew who He was and what He was sent to accomplish. He was the incarnate Son of the great "I Am" (Exodus 3:14), and while the religious leaders and others debated His identity, He was busy identifying with His Father, saying things like: "I am the bread of life" (John 6:35); "I am the light of the world" (John 8:12); "I am the way, the truth, and the life" (John 14:6).

Jesus clearly stated that His most important purpose was "to do the will of God who sent me" (John 6:38). Those of us in twelve-step recovery programs recognize this as the essence of step three. The Gospels record that He repeated this statement often when questioned about His motives for ministry. His awareness of His divine purpose began as early as age twelve when He expressed surprise at His earthly parents' lack of understanding that He "had to be" in His Father's house (Luke 2:49 NASB). Early in His ministry, He went to the synagogue in Nazareth and read Isaiah 61:1-2 to the congregation, the mission statement for His life: to preach good news to the poor, to proclaim freedom for those in captivity, to restore the sight of the blind, to release the oppressed, and to declare God's favor (Luke 4:16-19). Jesus viewed His purpose simply: to do good deeds and save life (Luke 6:9). He was in the world to work and the Gospels record how He rolled up the sleeves of His tunic and got busy.

It was this clear sense of purpose that allowed Jesus to defy accepted cultural and religious conventions. As He moved through His life, we find Him touching lepers (Luke 5:13), talking to a Samaritan woman (John 4:9), healing on the Sabbath (John 5:9), and, worst of all, being the guest of "those people," the sinners (Matthew 9:10-11). He was criticized for doing all of these, yet He didn't allow it to disturb His sense of serenity. He realized that popularity was fleeting—one day the crowds were singing His praises and the next they were driving Him out of town. He didn't allow the approval or disapproval of others to dictate His behavior because He knew He had God's approval, and that was what truly concerned Him. This confidence was so evident in His character that even the difficult to impress Pharisees remarked, "You aren't swayed by others" (Matthew 22:16 NIV). People mattered greatly to Jesus, but their opinions about Him did not. Free of the fear of disapproval, He could afford to speak honestly and truthfully to the people He encountered. It was just the kind of truth they needed to hear if they were to experience freedom.

Being sure of His identity and purpose allowed Jesus to set boundaries and take unpopular stands. Luke 4:42 says that after ministering in a certain town, the enamored people tried to keep Him there, but He refused because God's purpose for Him was to carry the message to other towns also, not bask in the praise of people. John's gospel records that He even set boundaries with His own family, risking their displeasure by refusing to accept their unsolicited career advice (John 7:1-9). He never allowed anything to come between Himself and God's purpose—at one point rebuking one of His closest disciples for inadvertently attempting to sidetrack Him from His mission (Matthew 16:21-23). Regardless of how much harassment, controversy, or evil plagued Him, He was never swayed from His purpose. Whether tempted by Satan in the wilderness while lonely, hungry, and tired (Matthew 4:1-4); endangered by the murderous plots and intrigues of the religious authorities (Matthew 26:1-5), or abandoned by His closest friends on the eve of His execution (Mark 14:50), He remained on course, determined to finish the work His Father in heaven had given Him.

Jesus "took" the world with love and acceptance. While He was a man on a mission, His motivation was love for people. Because He was able to love unconditionally, He had the ability to accept people as they were. Having been with God during humankind's creation and fall, He witnessed the devastating toll sin caused from a spiritual perspective. As He stood at the grave of His friend Lazarus and wept, He felt the devastation from a human perspective. He realized that everyone was suffering from the disease of sin and therefore in need of a physician. He understood that the result of sin was to render life "messy," and He wasn't afraid to wade right into the messiness of other people's lives. In fact, *The Message* version of John 1:14 says, "The Word became flesh and blood and moved into the neighborhood."

Jesus was fully engaged in the lives of others. He wasn't put off by their sickness, nor did He expect sick people to act any other way than sick. On the contrary, Hebrews 4:15 indicates that He was empathetic toward the weaknesses of people. He looked past the powerful, in-control façades that they presented and recognized that they were actually harassed and helpless—much more like sheep in need of a shepherd than masters of their own destiny (Matthew 9:36). His recognition of their true state of frailty served to increase His capacity for acceptance and compassion. He realized that His disciples were at times petty and competitive; that Peter was often brash and impulsive; that the tax collectors were mostly greedy scoundrels; and that despite their declarations of loyalty and good intentions, all of His disciples would desert Him. Because He understood that these "unacceptable" behaviors had fear at their core, He did not become frustrated, resentful, or take them personally. It was exactly why they needed a Savior. He placed principle above personality and loved people in spite of their character defects and failures.

The kind of love that Jesus demonstrated during His ministry on earth transformed people. John the apostle is a good example of this. It is interesting that in his gospel account he referred to himself not as the disciple who loved Jesus, but instead as the disciple Jesus loved (John 13:23). As a result of the love he received from Jesus, John was transformed from a punitive, egotistical "son of thunder" into a humble, gracious man who authored a New Testament epistle that repeatedly stressed the importance of sincerely loving others.

As I reflect upon Jesus' ability to patiently love people (including me) in their sickness, I recognize that too often it is my own inability to accept people as they are that disrupts my sense of serenity. Too often I find myself angry because the alcoholic is drinking, the liar is dishonest, and the irresponsible one is undependable. My anger does little to motivate them toward health, my frustration fails to leave room for God's grace, and they both do much to undermine my serenity. Jesus recognized the problem was sin, not people. And while He loved and accepted sick people, He wasn't content to simply leave them that way. He understood that it was the power of God's love and grace that motivated people toward health—not nagging, scolding, and lecturing. That's why He spent the majority of His time informing them that the good news for diseased people was that God was with them and for them and wanted to heal their diseases by accomplishing within them what they could not do for themselves. His message was that God's grace defied human logic, which is exactly what made it so amazing.

Jesus "took" the world with a clear understanding that the inner conditions of people were of more concern than the outer conditions of the world. A common misconception about Jesus is that He came to bring peace to the world, when in fact He came to bring peace to the inner person. He realized that what was in a person's heart would be translated into behavior (Luke 6:45). Character, beliefs, and motives were important to Him. He understood that people often pay lip service to principles while failing to apply them to their life (Matthew 15:8). Practicing God's principles was so important to Jesus that He likened it to building a house on a solid foundation (Luke 6:46-49). His most pointed criticisms were directed at the Pharisees because they failed to "walk the talk." Their performance-oriented behavior was motivated by arrogance and the desire to look better than others, rather than love for God and people. They were doing the right things for the wrong reasons. They may have looked "good" on the outside, but they weren't "well" on the inside. In the first oxymoron recorded in Scripture, Jesus referred to them as "blind guides" (Matthew 23:24). In recovery terms, they were in a state of denial with regard to the true state of their spiritual condition. While they worked hard to appear religiously fit on the outside, Jesus described their inner condition as being full of hypocrisy, wickedness, and dead men's bones. What they lacked was justice, mercy, and faithfulness—in other words, character (Matthew 23:1-28).

Jesus "took" the world with a servant's heart. He was quite simply born to give, telling His followers that He had come to serve others rather than be served (Matthew 20:28). He recognized that service to others brought light into a dark world and praise to His Father in heaven (Matthew 5:16). Those of us who struggle with codependency realize that too often we are giving to others out of fear, obligation, or guilt; in other words, our motivation for giving is wrong. Many times we are giving in order to get something in return—love, approval, status. Scripture is clear that God wants us to be cheerful givers (2 Corinthians 9:7). When done for any reason other than love, our giving will leave us feeling resentful rather than blessed. In contrast, Jesus gave with no ulterior motives. Scripture tells us that He gave because He was moved to compassion. While the crowds of followers were trying to suppress the two blind men's noisy attempts to attract His attention, Jesus was moved to compassion instead and healed them (Matthew 20:29-34). While still in the grip of grief over the death of His cousin John, Jesus was moved to compassion and healed a crowd of people (Mark 6:32-34). To Jesus, compassionate giving meant sacrificial giving.

Because it was compassionate giving, it was based on an understanding of what the person truly needed. Jesus wasn't a "one size fits all" God, but dealt with people according to their individual needs. This is reflected in His various approaches to healing people—sometimes asking them to verbalize what they wanted, sometimes requiring that they do something in order to be healed, sometimes simply touching them. He didn't give in ways that enabled their sickness as evidenced by His interaction with the cripple at the pool of Bethesda. He healed him in spite of his excuses, but sternly warned him that what he really needed more than physical healing was a change of lifestyle (John 5:1-15).

Jesus gave willingly, He gave joyfully, and He gave sacrificially. We never hear Him complaining that He was overworked or underappreciated. We never hear Him say, "I'm sorry. I'm on my way to an important meeting in Capernaum and I don't have time to heal you right now." On the contrary, His philosophy was, "My Father is always working, and so am I" (John 5:17). Even as He was breathing His final breaths, He was giving to others—dispensing forgiveness to the criminal at His side and arranging for the care of His mother after His death. And with His final breath as the Son of Man, He finished the work He was sent to do and gave the world the greatest gift of all. To this day He continues serving as He intercedes with God on behalf of His believers (1 John 2:1).

Taking the world as Jesus did means that I follow His example in setting my priorities, praying for guidance, understanding my purpose, valuing the internal, practicing love and acceptance, and serving others. As I reflect on all these examples, I am aware that taking the world as Jesus did is just what I am attempting to do by working the twelve steps of recovery. Step three says that we surrender our will and life to God, making it clear that God needs to be the number one priority in our lives. Step four encourages us to look deeply and considerately into our character, motives, and behavior. Putting love into practice by taking responsibility for our contribution to relationship problems and attempting to repair the damage is the focus of steps eight and nine. In step eleven we are encouraged to use prayer to gain not only guidance and knowledge regarding our purpose, but the power to translate it into behavior. And giving to others from a place of gratitude is the essence of step twelve.

As we make a commitment to move through our world, practicing the same principles that Jesus evidenced during His ministry, we cannot help but experience the same serenity that was so characteristic of His life.

Deborah Galasso

"Taking as Jesus Did" and Me

When I was a little girl attending Sunday school, my favorite part of the morning was singing all those songs about Jesus—especially the ones with hand motions. It was my first introduction to theology, and through their simple messages I discovered that Jesus loved me, all the children of the world, and a wee little man named Zacchaeus! As a result of those songs I learned very early in life that Jesus loved people, and in turn, I loved Him.

When I became older I began to read the Gospels for myself, but I found it hard to relate to the Jesus of the Gospels. I'm not sure why this was so, but my interpretation of the descriptions of Him made Him seem distant and detached. I pictured Him moving through the world, bathed in a holy light that rendered Him untouchable by mere humans. When He said things like "Oh, you of little faith" I heard condemnation and judgment rather than love and concern.

Fortunately, my inaccurate perceptions concerning Jesus were corrected by two things. The first was a book written by Phillip Yancey called *The Jesus I Never Knew*. Within the pages of that book all of my ideas about Jesus were challenged, and by the time I finished reading it my rather one-dimensional concept had been replaced with a more complete understanding of the complexity and character of Jesus. The second thing that changed my view point of Jesus was watching Bruce Marchiano's portrayal of Jesus in the movie *Matthew*. Every word He spoke on screen was verbatim from Matthew's gospel, so I had read those words many times before. What was different was that I hadn't *heard* those words before. The way in which Jesus was presented left no doubt that he was fully engaged with, and completely passionate about, people. When Bruce Marchiano's Jesus said the words, "Oh, you of little faith," it was with an expression of kind concern for, and patient understanding of, the human condition—not the indictment that I had mistakenly interpreted it to be. In fact, I once heard Bruce explain during a talk he gave at our church that when Jesus preached "repent," "it was a joyous invitation to the joy of salvation and freedom from sin, not heavy-handed condemnation."[37]

The combination of these two factors altered my notion of Jesus drastically, resulting in a renewed ability to love and appreciate Him and a genuine desire to evidence His character in my life. This change in perception was essential to my serenity because it provided the foundation on which I could work the principle of "taking as Jesus did." Certain aspects of His actions seemed quite easy to emulate. I wholeheartedly agreed with the concept of making God the highest priority in my life. I was sold on the importance of prayer as the way to improve my conscious contact with God. I acknowledged that my primary purpose in this life was to do God's will. These were all things I could embrace because they involved me alone.

It was when "taking as Jesus did" involved loving people that I fell regrettably short. Jesus was a people person, and if I wanted to follow in His steps then I would need to become people oriented also. That was not a prospect I relished, because being task oriented was so much more efficient and invulnerable. Never mind that this approach was a lot like that of the Pharisees; it seemed safer nonetheless. Developing the character of Jesus required that I accept others just as they were. Desiring His character meant that I evidenced the same compassion for people that He displayed. I wanted to love and accept people the way Jesus did, but I just couldn't seem to. I didn't know how to accept the person while rejecting their sin. I had a hard time remembering that it was possible to love people even when they evidenced disease. My giving to others was too often motivated by fear, obligation, or guilt, and rarely by the empathy that characterized the charity of Jesus. I was too often too full of myself, which left me with little room for loving others.

Jesus identified love for others as the second greatest commandment, not the second greatest option. God wants me to love others because love has the potential to be a powerful healing force in an ailing world. I have experienced firsthand the healing power of love as a result of my relationship with my good friend Donna, who happens to be one of the most loving people I know. There is hardly ever a time when I talk to her that she doesn't say, "Deborah, I love you." The healing impact of those words is difficult to describe. Given that she knows the majority of my former secrets, her expressions of love for me are that much more meaningful as well as healing. This is the kind of healing power that God wants to dispense into a hurting world through my willing attempts to love others.

The love that Jesus gave to others had the power to heal, precisely because it was a love that was always patient, kind, humble, considerate, unselfish, longsuffering, forgiving, pure, honest, protecting, trusting, hopeful, persevering, and unfailing. It was, and continues to be, "the most excellent way" referred to in the thirteenth chapter of First Corinthians. There is only one word to describe that kind of love—divine. And so in my ongoing struggle to love others I realize this truth: the only way that I can love others with that type of love is as Christ's Spirit loves them through me. To take as Jesus did, to love as Jesus loved, requires the love of Jesus. As with every other area of deficiency in my life, the solution is always the same: I can't, He can, so I let Him. As I continue to practice this simple process, I am empowered to love others.

Interestingly enough, I find that the uncomplicated theology of my childhood continues to serve me well in my attempts to live out the principles of the Serenity Prayer today. Because of my belief in the truth of a simple Sunday school song—that Jesus loves me—I can take this world with love just as He did.

"Taking as Jesus Did" and You

1. Which aspect of how Jesus "took" the world would you most like to emulate?

2. Are you satisfied with where you have placed God in terms of your priorities? What plausible excuses prevent you from giving God the number one position in your life?

3. If you were to write a mission statement for your life, how would it read?

4. How can having a clear sense of identity and purpose aid your recovery?

5. In what situations and with which people do you experience difficulty speaking honestly and truthfully? Are there truths that you are withholding that need to be shared?

6. How are you expressing compassion and acceptance for the people in your life in spite of their shortcomings and failures?

7. How's your prayer life?

8. How are you following the example of Jesus with regard to serving others? What benefits have you experienced as a result of this?

9. How has focusing on character development influenced your serenity?

10. What did Jesus teach regarding the importance of giving God highest priority in this life and recognizing Him as the source of all things? (Matthew 6:7-8, 24, 26; Mark 6:8; Luke 10:21; Luke 11-11-13; John 5:19; John 8:28; John 14:12-14, 28; John 17:4)

11. What did Jesus say about His identity and purpose? (Matthew 5:17; Luke 19:10; John 6:35, 38-40, 51; John 7:16; John 8:12; John 10:7, 10-11, 30; John 11:25; John 14:6; John 14:9-14)

12. What do the following Scriptures reveal about why service was important to Jesus? (Matthew 20:25-28; Luke 6:38; John 9:4; John 12:26; John 13:14-17; Philippians 2:5-11)

13. What do the following Scriptures tell you about whom Jesus showed compassion to and how He demonstrated it? (Matthew 9:36; Matthew 14:14; Matthew 15:32; Matthew 20:34; Mark 1:40-42; Luke 7:12-15; Luke 19:41-42; John 11:32-35)

14. What does Scripture reveal about when Jesus prayed, for whom He prayed, and what He taught about prayer? (Matthew 5:44; Matthew 14:23; Matthew 21:22; Matthew 26:41; Mark 1:35; Mark 11:24; Luke 5:16; Luke 6:12-13; Luke 6:28; Luke 11:2-4; Luke 18:1; John 17:1-2; John 17:15)

15. Read John 17:20. How does knowing that Jesus prayed for you affect your commitment to prayer?

---

16. What did Jesus say about character versus appearance? (Matthew 6:2-3; Matthew 6:5-6; Matthew 6:16-18; Matthew 15:11, 18-20; Matthew 23:5-6; Matthew 23:25-28; John 7:24)

---

17. What "hard to hear" truths does Scripture indicate Jesus expressed? Which of these are the hardest for you to hear? (Matthew 18:3-4; Matthew 19:23-24; Matthew 21:21-22; Matthew 21:28-32; Matthew 25:1-13,34-46; Luke 14:25-27; John 3:3; John 8:34; John 12:24)

---

18. What reactions to His message and behavior did Jesus experience, and what was His response? (Matthew 12:1-8, 22-24; Matthew 15:1-14; Matthew 22:15-22, 34; Matthew 26:62-68; Mark 2:15-18; Mark 3:1-6; Mark 6:47; Luke 4:16-30; Luke 13:31-33; John 4:27; John 5:16-18; John 7:1-9, 19-24, 40-44; John 10:31-33)

---

19. How can knowing that Jesus faced such opposition and unpopularity aid your recovery?

20. What idea from this chapter do you plan to put into practice?

Chapter Thirteen: This Sinful World as It Is

I frequently have to remind myself that this road of recovery on which I am traveling is winding its way through a sinful world, not a recovering world. I have the tendency to forget that I am the one in recovery, while this sinful world is not. When I forget this reality, it becomes all too easy to conform to "this sinful world as it is" rather than simply accept it as it is. Because the prevailing belief system of the world is often in direct conflict to the principles of both Scripture as well as the Serenity Prayer, the ability to experience serenity will depend upon how I resolve this conflict.

Every day through the media we receive all kinds of messages from the sinful world which influence our beliefs and behavior. We are led to believe that with more money, advanced technology, or the correct political party problems such as poverty, violence, and war can be eliminated. We are influenced to believe that if we reduce pollution by driving less, recycling more, and eliminating plastic grocery bags, we can "save the planet." The message is clear—we have the power, ability, and obligation to change the world and create a kind of utopia on earth. As I unwittingly fall under the influence of these beliefs and yet witness the worsening of society's problems in spite of our diligent efforts, it is easy to throw up my hands in outrage or disillusionment and well...there goes my serenity.

Please don't get me wrong. I am all for wanting to do my part to act responsibly with regard to the environment, respond compassionately to the needs of others, and contribute conscientiously to the improvement of the world I inhabit. The problem with the prevailing philosophies of this sinful world is that they fail to recognize the limitations of human effort alone and at times are downright inaccurate. Chief among these inaccuracies is the notion that this world isn't a sinful place at all, but rather a good place, getting better all the time.

In spite of our best efforts, the reality for our planet as described in Scripture is that "the earth will wear out like a piece of clothing" (Isaiah 51:6). Paul explained that all of nature is in a state of decay and ongoing decline that was introduced when sin entered the world (Romans 8:20-22). As well-meaning as our efforts to preserve our environment may be, ultimately they will fail to arrest environmental problems, because, while the problem is indeed one of pollution, it is actually the pollution of sinfulness which lies at the root of humankind's problems. Sadly, the Bible teaches that the world will continue its downward spiral because that is the nature and course of sin.

You may be thinking that for a book about serenity, this chapter seems like a real downer so far—all doom and gloom. But as recovering people seeking serenity, we must have an accurate perspective concerning this sinful world in order to practice what the Serenity Prayer advises and take it "as it is." As long as we are trying to conform to world philosophies that are in direct conflict to God's Word and the principles of recovery, it will be difficult to experience serenity. Living serenity depends upon a commitment to rigorous honesty and truth. There can be no lasting experience of serenity if we are conforming to mistaken beliefs.

Acquiring an accurate perspective depends upon understanding how biblical truth and popular world philosophy differ. Paul warned us, "See to it that no one takes you captive through hollow and deceptive philosophy, which depends on human tradition and the elemental spiritual forces of this world rather than on Christ" (Colossians 2:8 NIV). More often than not, the principles of this world and the principles of Christ stand in stark contrast to each other. Paul tells us that there is no substance to the world's philosophy, and even worse we can become trapped by its deceitfulness. The thing about deceit is that it is subtle. It is a lot like denial. We don't realize we are being deceived until after we are deceived. It happens gradually over time as we are exposed repeatedly to prevailing world opinion.

Contrary to the idea that the world is a good place getting better all the time, Ephesians 6:12 (NIV) describes the world as "dark." Jesus used some pretty dark words to describe the world when He called it "pagan" (Luke 12:30 NIV), "shrewd" (Luke 16:8), and full of hate (John 15:18). And if those descriptions weren't quite dark enough, Paul added that the world is condemned (1 Corinthians 11:32), gradually passing away (1 Corinthians 7:31), and a prisoner of sin (Galatians 3:22 NIV).

In a word, the world is broken. It was not always broken. There was a time when the world actually was good. If we go back to the book of beginnings, we see that as God created the world, He pronounced each aspect of His creation, including people, "good" (Genesis 1:4-31). However, as a result of Adam and Eve's decision to exercise their freedom to choose against God's will, sin entered the picture, bringing brokenness with it. Through sin, relationship with God was broken, relationship with each other was broken, and relationship with the world was broken. The state of humankind, as well as the world, was no longer "good." Sin changed everything. Romans 8:20-21 tells us that creation was subjected to a curse as a result of the fall and is waiting to be freed from its subjection to death and decay. So much for the idea that the world is a good place getting better all the time!

If we are to do as the Serenity Prayer says and take "this sinful world as it is," then in addition to having an accurate perspective of the world, it is also helpful to have an accurate understanding of the concept of sin. One common misunderstanding people share with regard to sin is the failure to appreciate its power. We tend to think of sin as simply being a harmless mistake or transgression, when actually it is a powerful force which operates in the world and produces far-reaching consequences. It is important to realize that ultimately sin always produces negative consequences. Just look at some of the words that are associated with sin: "disgrace" (Proverbs 14:34); "wicked" (Proverbs 29:16); "hinders" (Hebrews 12:1 NIV); "wrath" (Ephesians 2:3 NASB); "wrongdoing" (1 John 5:17 NIV);

and "lawlessness" (1 John 3:4 NASB). We are told that we "struggle" with it (Hebrews 12:4), that it can hinder our progress, (Hebrews 12:1 NIV) and that we can become "trapped" by it (Proverbs 29:6). I don't know about you, but for me, none of these words conjure up a picture of serenity.

The Bible is clear that sin wants to be the driving force in our lives. Romans 6:12 states that sin wants to "control" us; Psalm 119:133 indicates that sin wants to "overcome" us; and Romans 6:14 says that it wants to "master" us. The idea of mastering sin goes all the way back to one of the earliest sins recorded in the Bible, that of Cain killing Abel. Before Cain carried out his malicious intention toward his brother, God warned Cain of the power of sin and the need to be on guard against it when He said, "...sin is crouching at your door; it desires to have you, but you must rule over it" (Genesis 4:7 NIV). Sadly, Cain failed to understand not only what a powerful force he was dealing with, but also the far-reaching consequences it would produce. As a result of his sin, Cain became a homeless outcast who wandered the earth.

And that is the problem with sin: it always has negative consequences which we do not anticipate. Sometimes these consequences accompany the sin, but many times they do not and can only be realized in the future. It is doubtful that Eve understood, as she took the first bite of that innocent-looking fruit, the way in which her world would be turned upside down. Or that Abraham realized that the decision to father a child with Hagar would conceive a religious conflict which exists to the present day. Or that David foresaw the mayhem that would visit his family for generations when he sent for Bathsheba that night. To Eve it was just a nice-looking piece of fruit, to Abraham it was just a way to appease his wife, and to David it was just a one night stand.

The Bible is clear that whether we anticipate these consequences or not, sin can eventually enslave (Romans 6:6), imprison (Galatians 3:22) and hold us captive (Acts 8:23). Just like the addictions it breeds, the nature of sin is chronic, progressive, and terminal. Throughout the book of Romans, Paul talked about people's "sinful nature" which substantiates the chronic essence of sin. In fact,

Scripture taken as a whole presents a picture of the enduring nature of sin and humankind's need to be delivered from it. Those of us who struggle with addiction understand the implications of living with a chronic condition. It does not go away; it can only be managed on a day-by-day, moment-by-moment basis. It is interesting that the term "craving," which is associated with addiction, is also associated with sin. Ephesians 2:3 (NIV) states: "All of us also lived among them at one time, gratifying the cravings of our flesh and following its desires and thoughts…."

This leads us to another aspect of sin, which is that it is progressive. Just as in the case of untreated addiction, sin tends to worsen over time. James 1:14-15 discusses the progressive nature of sin which evolves from temptation to desire to sinful acts. Jeremiah 9:3 (NIV) talks about going "from one sin to another." Paul lamented that sin had the power to produce all kinds of harmful desires in him (Romans 7:8). Unfortunately, sin doesn't remain in a steady state; it tends to worsen without intervention.

The most dreadful characteristic of addictive disease is that it is terminal. Without successful treatment it will eventually result in some type of death, whether physical, spiritual, social, or emotional. This is true for sin as well. Scripture makes it very clear that the result of sin is death. In one of the most quoted passages of Scripture, Romans 6:23 says, "For the wages of sin is death." And James 1:15 (NIV) echoes this truth when it says, "and sin, when it is full-grown, gives birth to death." While we most often associate sin with spiritual death, sin can produce death in a variety of other ways. For instance, sin can contribute to the death of relationships or the "deadening" of our emotions.

Sin has a profound ability to affect our serenity because it affects us on every level of our being. First Peter 2:11 tells us that sin fights against our souls, which speaks to the fact that sin affects the whole person; it is a whole-person disease. We erroneously think of sin as simply a spiritual problem, but the truth is that sin has the potential to affect us on all levels—physical, mental, emotional, and social—in addition to spiritual. Psalm 38 paints a picture of mental and physical distress caused by sin which includes acute pain, exhaustion, guilt, grief, and anguish of heart. Proverbs 17:19 indicates that sin can affect us on a social level as it is associated with interpersonal conflict. Throughout the Bible, sin is connected with the condition referred to as hard-heartedness. People with this condition are desensitized, not just to God, but to people as well. Pharaoh showed no compassion for the adversity of the Israelite slaves because his heart was hardened (Exodus 7:13). Jesus indicated that divorce was associated with a hardened heart (Matthew 19:8). Having our emotions hardened by sin results in problems for both ourselves and others.

When the Serenity Prayer refers to "this sinful world as it is," it is referring to all of the above. We are exposed to all of this and more—day in and day out. Sin is toxic to our whole being and we can become poisoned by association. This is one of the reasons that recovery focuses on a lifestyle change rather than abstinence alone. Proverbs 22:24-25 indicates that we can inadvertently absorb things simply through ongoing association. And Peter used the word "tormented" to describe the effects of chronic exposure to sinful behavior in the world (2 Peter 2:8 NASB). As recovering people, we must never forget that we are living in a toxic environment. When we fail to remember this truth, it is like forgetting to open the windows to ventilate the room when we are spraying insecticide—it can genuinely harm us. James 1:27 (NIV) warns us to "keep oneself from being polluted by the world." By understanding the serious hazards of association with sin, we can be motivated to avoid willing participation in it, which in turn arrests the perpetuation of its negative consequences.

Learning how to live a principled life in an unprincipled world is an ongoing challenge for people desiring serenity. It is what Jesus had in mind when He discussed with His disciples the importance of living in the world without becoming like the world (John 17:15-16). The principles that lead to serenity, which we are attempting to practice in all areas of our lives, will often be in direct opposition to the accepted standards of the world. The world honors fame, fortune, and power, while God honors humility. The world places a high value on externals such as beauty, possessions, and achievements, while God values internals such as character, attitude, and faith. Lack of accountability and blame seem to be the order of the day in the sinful world, while God encourages us to examine ourselves instead. While the principles of the sinful world encourage covering up through deceit and shrewdness, God encourages owning up by admitting mistakes and seeking truth. Jesus referred to this contrast when He pointed out that His people had a distinct disadvantage in the world because godly people are not as shrewd as the streetwise people of the world (Luke 16:8)

To guard our serenity in a sinful world we must approach the sinful world with our eyes open, keeping in mind the truth of Colossians 2:20 (NASB) which reminds us that we have died to the basic principles of this world. This means that we don't succumb to the pressure to fit in by condoning, conforming, or apologizing. Peter said that we are foreigners and aliens in this world (1 Peter 2:11). Guess what? We are not supposed to fit in. This sinful world is simply a temporary home. We are spiritual beings housed in human bodies who are just passing through. Internalizing this truth has been of immense comfort to a misfit like me. All my life I struggled in an attempt to fit in. Now, in recovery, I find that I wasn't supposed to fit in anyway!

While this chapter has discussed the idea of a "sinful world," the reality is that sin does not reside in the world; it resides in the hearts of people. My efforts to create a better world are much more effective when I begin with confronting the pollution of my own heart. It is only as individual hearts change that a sinful world becomes a hopeful world. As He prepared to leave this sinful world, Christ encouraged His disciples with the words, "But take heart, because I have overcome the world" (John 16:33). Through relationship with Christ, we do not have to succumb to the effects of this sinful world, but can instead overcome them. Embracing this heartening truth encourages us to continue our journey through this sinful world with an attitude of hope and serenity.

"This Sinful World as It Is" and Me

When I find that my serenity is fading, there are two simple words that more often than not will restore my serenity in an instant: "sinful world." It is the shorthand version of "What do you expect from a sinful world, Deborah?" and it reminds me to check my expectations. If I fail to do this, I am on course to run my serenity aground with my unrealistic expectations for the sinful world, and then there I am—shipwrecked on the Isle of Resentment!

It is pretty easy to become a castaway. I head in that direction when I expect the world to be fair and just. Or when I feel I am being treated unfairly or criticized unjustly. For a people-pleasing codependent like me, insensitive treatment in the form of unkindness, criticism, or rejection is both surprising and unpleasant. It doesn't feel good to be disliked without good reason. In fact, it doesn't even feel good to be disliked *with* good reason.

I remember a situation in my life when I was saying "sinful world" to myself so often it was practically a chant. We were involved in a financial dispute with a trusted business associate. In spite of efforts to settle the matter without legal intervention, the case proceeded to court. This involved hiring an attorney at considerable cost. The case dragged on for a number of years until it reached the point where it had to either be settled or dismissed. The day we went to trial, the lawyers settled the case in the courthouse hallway prior to appearing before the judge.

I struggled with resentment throughout the whole process. I resented the business associate because, in my opinion, his demands were unreasonable. I resented the lawyers for dragging the case out for years while collecting fees every fifteen minutes. I especially resented that, after collecting those fees, they were able to settle the case so rapidly at the courthouse instead of during the many hours of conference room meetings that preceded the court date. I resented my husband for involving himself in a business venture with this person, and I resented colleagues who appeared to take the other person's side. I had enough vexation to build a large condo complex and take up residency on the Isle of Resentment.

The only way out was to remember that it was all related to life in a sinful world where things, as well as people, are not just, fair, or reasonable. I had to realize that it was okay to be perplexed and have the breath knocked out of me by sin, but I didn't have to be overcome by it, which is exactly what ongoing resentment and bitterness would do to me. I felt hurt and frustrated, but I didn't have to feel hopeless or destroyed. When I felt overwhelmed, I meditated on the fact that Christ had overcome the sinful world, and that through Him I could too. That thought never failed to restore my sanity as well as my serenity.

When the case was finally settled, God's justice prevailed and it was settled for the original offer we had proposed. I do not know why we had to go through such a seemingly futile situation, but I do know that I learned a lot about the sinful world and myself in the process. I learned that if I rely on God's help to overcome the effects of sin, I don't have to succumb to becoming like the world by operating in the darkness of resentment, bitterness, and retaliation. I can instead experience gratitude for His blessings, even in the midst of sinful, unfair situations.

Saying the words "sinful world" reminds me to consider the source. As I look at the people in my world, I see many who are operating under the influence of one addiction or another. Only a fraction of them participate in an ongoing program of recovery. It is unrealistic for me to expect people without a program to practice principles of which they have no knowledge. And it certainly does not make sense to trade my serenity for resentment in response to another person's unawareness.

While some people are under the influence of addiction, everyone is under the influence of sin. Sinful people do sinful things. And the truth is that I am as sinful as the next person. The only difference is that I have availed myself of a program of recovery from not just the effects of addiction, but the effects of sin as well. I am learning to stop personalizing the sinful behavior of others by reminding myself that their behavior is not about me, but rather a function of their sinful nature. While this does not change the fact that unkind behavior directed at me still hurts—I'm still a codependent for heaven's sake!—I have to ask myself: "Do I want to add to the hurt by trading my serenity for resentment?"

I am comforted when I realize that Christ was one of the most misunderstood people who ever lived, and He was perfect. I often have to remind myself that when I am being criticized or treated negatively it does not necessarily mean that I have done something wrong. Living in this sinful world requires that I diligently use all the tools of my recovery program, as well as my Christian faith, to prevent myself from internalizing negative messages. I can instead choose to replace them with those that further my growth and character development.

Thankfully, I don't vacation on the Isle of Resentment as often as I used to. In the past I was there so often I had a standing reservation; now, I just end up there on occasion. And when I realize where I've landed, you can bet I'm quoting the Serenity Prayer while moving quickly toward the dock, looking for the next sailboat out.

"This Sinful World as It Is" and You

1. What is the sin that so easily entangles you, and when are you most vulnerable to entanglement?

2. Are there "basic principles of this world" that you struggle with? What biblical principles can you apply to each?

3. What physical, mental, emotional, social, and spiritual consequences have you experienced as a result of sin?

4. In what ways have you experienced sin's tendency to be progressive, chronic, and terminal?

5. What descriptive words are associated with sin and the sinful world in the following Scriptures? (Psalm 38: 3, 5, 18; Proverbs 5:22; Acts 8:23; Romans 6:16; 1 Corinthians 11:32; Galatians 4:3; Philippians 2:15; Hebrews 11:25; 1 John 3:4)

6. What consequences do the following Scriptures identify as accompanying sin? (Numbers 32:23; Psalm 66:18; Psalm 106:43; Isaiah 30:12-13; John 8:34; Romans 5:12)

7. What warnings does Scripture give regarding living in the sinful world? Which of these are most applicable to your struggles? (Mark 9:43-47; Luke 12:29-30; 1 Corinthians 7:29-31; Galatians 5:1, 19-21; James 4:4; 2 Peter 2:20; 1 John 2:15-17; 1 John 3:13; 1 John 5:19)

8. How does what you have "in Christ" contrast with what is "in the world"? (John 7:38; John 12:44-46; John 14:12; John 15:4-7; John 16:33; Ephesians 2:12; 2 Peter 1:4; 1 John 2:16; 1 John 4:3)

9. According to the following Scriptures, what is the solution for bringing hope to this sinful world? (2 Chronicles 7:14; Psalm 32:5; Psalm 119:11; Micah 7:18-19; John 1:29; Romans 5:20-21; Romans 8:3-4; 1 John 4:4; 1 John 5:4-5)

10. What idea from this chapter do you plan to put into practice?

Chapter Fourteen: Not as I Would Have It

If I could have the world my way, it would be just that—my way. Everyone would agree with my ideas, people would do things the way I think they should be done, and there would seldom be rainy days, because I prefer blue skies and sunshine rather than all that gray. It would be a great world, at least for me. Of course, you might not like it too much because my idea of what constitutes a great world and your idea of that are probably quite different. And then there is the whole problem of what all that sunshine without rain might do to the ecosystem! And that is the problem with wanting the world to be my way. It really would not work as well as I think it would. Because if I am rigorously honest about the kind of world I want, I would have to admit that I want the world to revolve around me.

The psychological term for this kind of thinking is "egocentric," which means self-centered or selfish. The recovery term for it is "self-will run riot." It is the "I, self, me" that twelve-step programs refer to as the "ism" in alcoholism. Simply put, it is "me" at the center of everything. It is the condition in which all humans begin life in this world. As infants born in a helpless, dependent state, we are completely egocentric and the world really does revolve around us. We cry when we are in need, and someone responds. And if they fail to respond, our survival instincts kick in to insure that we keep right on crying until they do. Anyone who has heard the persistent, escalating cry of a newborn understands what I am talking about.

As we successfully grow and mature, we learn that we are not the only people on the world stage, and our egocentrism is gradually replaced by a sense of community and interrelatedness. We learn that we have needs and others do also. We develop the ability to compromise, delay gratification, and meet one another's needs—important life skills which not only allow us to live in harmony with others, but also enhance our ability to experience serenity.

Yet regardless of our maturity level, to a greater or lesser extent, that primal tendency toward egocentricity will always be there. In my most vulnerable, fearful, or traumatic moments, I will tend to regress to preservation of the self—me, first and foremost. People cannot completely get away from self-centeredness because it is a function of both our God-given survival instincts as well as our sinful nature. As we learned in the previous chapter, sin entered the world because of humankind's desire to have self rather than God at the center of life, and that desire has been producing selfishness ever since. Because the problem of self first is the essence of our sinful nature, in this life we will always struggle with the issue of egocentricity.

The phrase "not as I would have it," reminds me that as I attempt to practice the Serenity Prayer, I will be challenged on a daily basis to subdue my tendency to act selfishly. If I wish to live a life characterized by serenity, I will have to pay particular attention to how selfishness manifests itself in my life. Like so many other character defects, I am often blinded to not only its existence, but also its consequences. Selfishness will interfere with my serenity because I was created to live in relationship with others. Christ identified the ability to care about the interests of others, as much as we care about our own, as the second most important commandment ever given (Matthew 22:39). Nothing disrupts this balanced interdependence that our Creator intended more than selfishness.

A common hiding place for selfishness is greed. Christ harshly criticized the Pharisees because of their character defects of greed and self-indulgence (Matthew 23:25). It is not hard to recognize that greed and self-indulgence often go hand in hand. Greed—the desire for more and more of something—and self-indulgence—gratification of our excessive desires—are the hallmark of any addictive process. Whether drinking, drugging, gambling, lusting, eating, spending, working, or rescuing those who did, we were committed to gratifying these desires "more and more." There was no price too high to pay and no consequence too harmful to endure in our drive to satisfy our addictions. And as a result, we experienced firsthand the utter lack of serenity which accompanies a life characterized by the greed and self-indulgence of the disease of "more and more."

Unfortunately, greed is not just associated with the problem of addiction. In today's world, greed and self-indulgence seem to be the norm rather than the exception. Power, money, and excessive living are readily endorsed and promoted in our society. This is reflected in the appeal of "reality" programming, which currently tends to dominate television. Regardless of how glamorously it may be disguised, greed has a darker side. Greed is at the root of some of the worst atrocities committed in our world today— murder, genocide, drug and human trafficking. It is no wonder Paul said, "The love of money is the root of all kinds of evil" (1 Timothy 6:10). In fact, almost all crime directed against others has its roots in greed.

Greed is not difficult to spot in such extreme cases; it is in its subtle forms that we are inclined to overlook it. Yet, like sin, greed has far-reaching, unanticipated effects for everyone it touches. Whether we perpetrate greed or are victimized by it, we all become casualties of greed because the most dangerous effect of greed is its ability to unravel and depersonalize relationships. In the pursuit to acquire more "things," relationships gradually become expendable, "things" become more important than people, and ultimately people become treated as "things." The effects of this kind of depersonalization on interpersonal relationships are serious and devastating. This is why even a little greed cannot be considered harmless. Living serenity requires that we resist the urge toward practicing greed and self-indulgence in our lives, regardless of how normal and pervasive they may appear in our culture.

Another form of selfishness which Scripture warns against is called selfish ambition. While it is admirable to eagerly pursue a goal, when that goal is motivated by selfish desire it can lead to problems. Paul identified "selfish ambition" as one of fifteen "acts of the flesh" which included things like orgies, witchcraft, and hatred (Galatians 5:19-20 NIV). Yikes! Put in that context, it doesn't seem quite so harmless! James 3:13-18 indicates that where selfish ambition is found disorder and every kind of evil practice will be found also. While at first glance James' description may seem radical, it is not hard to see that ambition and commitment when taken to the extreme become liabilities rather than positive characteristics. Intimidation, manipulation, and deception often become the tools by which overly ambitious people secure their success. Unfortunately, most of us can probably cite examples of people who engaged in unscrupulous behavior on their way to the top. In fact, for those of us recovering from work addiction, we may have been one of those people at one time! Even when we are acting in ethical ways, selfish ambition can still damage relationships by putting us at odds with others. For example, a little healthy competition may be good for the work environment, but when someone must always be number one, it can lead to obstructing the efforts of others which can't help but diminish teamwork and camaraderie over time.

Selfish ambition is not simply confined to work settings; we bring it into our personal relationships also. We do this by continually putting our own needs first while discounting the needs of others. Those of us in recovery must keep in mind that, when carried into our relationships, the self-gratification which was the hallmark of our addictions will undoubtedly cause problems. Relationships are meant to be mutually satisfying. When we are under the influence of selfish ambition, it cannot help but have a detrimental effect on relationships because we direct more effort toward meeting self-seeking goals than toward those that benefit the relationship. We fail to invest the necessary time or energy needed to nurture relationships with our children, spouses, and friends. And while loving relationships can absorb a certain amount of neglect necessitated by the drive to "get ahead," over a sustained period of time it impoverishes them.

At this juncture, people who struggle with codependency may be tempted to think that selfish ambition does not apply to them; after all, codependents are "giving" people, not selfish people. On the other hand, part of the problem in codependency is the tendency to believe that we know what is best for other people. It is just this belief that motivates our acts of "giving" without being solicited for help. This qualifies as a form of selfish ambition in that it is our ambition for someone, rather than their own. More often than not, we have more ambition for some of the people in our lives than they have for themselves. We can become as relentless and driven in the pursuit of the goal of changing people as any workaholic is about the pursuit of success. In the long run, these ambitious actions breed resentment, and while this may not be the "evil" that James referred to, resentment can certainly bring "disorder" to our relationships. It is impossible to have serene and fulfilling relationships with resentment draped all over them.

Because selfish behavior is so innate in our nature, subtle in its manifestations, and promoted by our culture, identifying it in our everyday lives will be challenging. Careful examination of our actions and motives is the only way to uncover it. This supports the importance of completing the searching moral inventory of ourselves recommended in twelve-step groups as well as an ongoing daily inventory of our actions toward others. These two disciplines cannot be considered optional for people who are serious about recovery. Scripture encourages us to "examine" ourselves (Lamentations 3:40). Thorough, considerate self-examination is the necessary tool for revealing not just selfish behavior, but also the damaging effects it has on others. As a result of this process, we can offer amends, preserve our relationships, prevent future problems, and promote serenity. While Scripture encourages examination, it does not encourage condemnation. As with all other character defects with which we struggle, God's grace covers any shortcomings we uncover with regard to selfishness. Our responsibility is to admit their presence and humbly ask Him to remove them.

The world is full of empty people attempting to fill their lives with material things through acts of greed, self-indulgence, and selfish ambition. In stark contrast to this, Jesus instructed us to put selfish ambition aside, shoulder our crosses, and follow Him (Matthew 16:24). Following Him means that we become committed to what He was committed to, namely service to others. When Jesus issued the challenge to Simon Peter to "follow me" (Matthew 4:19), He was inviting him not simply into the camaraderie of discipleship for a few years, but into a lifetime of service. Service to others, just like following, requires great humility—the kind of humility that led Christ to not just take up His cross, but to die on it also. Philippians 2:7-8 points out that Christ chose to make Himself nothing. He purposely emptied Himself of the majesty that was rightfully His so that, in humility and obedience, He could become the servant of all people. While the depth of humility demonstrated by Christ is almost inconceivable, it is through service to others that we begin to acquire genuine humility and learn to loosen our grip on self-centeredness. Service to others requires great humility; great humility is learned by serving others. What a curious relationship.

Humility is an important prerequisite to successful recovery. So many of the actions required by the twelve steps of recovery require humility—admitting we are powerless; turning our will and life over to God's care; evaluating our character defects and asking for them to be removed; as well as making amends. The Bible commends the virtue of humility and says that God saves, guides, sustains, elevates, and extends grace to people who evidence it. Jesus described Himself as "gentle and humble in heart" (Matthew 11:29 NASB). Moses, revered as one of the most important prophets of the Bible, was described as "more humble than any other person on earth" (Numbers 12:3). It is obvious that God values the characteristic of humility. Humble people are the channels through which He dispenses grace to an "ungraceful," selfish world. Peter encouraged us to use the gifts God had bestowed on us to serve others, because that is how God's grace is distributed to our world (1 Peter 4:10). Humility leads to service, and service enables God's grace to reach others.

On the other hand, pride leaves little room for God's grace to be dispersed. Obadiah 3 indicates that pride can be deceptive. Pride can lead to denial, which is a dangerous condition for a recovering person. Revelation 3:17 points out the relationship between pride and denial when it says, "You say, 'I am rich. I have everything I want. I don't need a thing!' And you don't realize that you are wretched and miserable and poor and blind and naked." When we operate under the influence of pride, we are unable to see our true condition. This inability to see, also known as denial, can set the stage for relapse.

Proverbs 16:18 warns that "pride goes before destruction, and haughtiness before a fall." When we are full of ourselves, we not only run the risk of a fall, but we also miss the opportunity to serve God's purposes.

Developing humility and learning to deny self does not mean that we abdicate the responsibility to care for ourselves. There is a distinction between selfishness and self-care. Contrary to much of the self-help literature on codependency, Scripture never encourages us to be selfish. It does encourage us to treat ourselves with the same level of regard that we treat others. This level of mutual regard is delineated in the "one another" Scriptures which encourage us to be kind, loving, comforting, forgiving, forbearing, compassionate, hospitable, and prayerful toward one another, to name just a few. To treat ourselves with the same compassion, kindness, and respect with which we treat others is not selfish. As we implement this level of regard in caring for ourselves, it may necessitate learning to say "no" and set boundaries which may feel like selfish acts. To care for self at the exclusion of others is selfish; to care for others at the exclusion of self is martyrdom. It is important to remind ourselves that caring for self and caring for others can be inclusive rather than exclusive.

Service is the antidote to selfishness. Romans 2:8-12 is clear that self-seeking behaviors will ultimately bring trouble and distress while doing good, which would include acts of service, will result in serenity. There are two types of people in the world: those who serve and those who want to be served. Jesus, the Prince of Peace—that is serenity—made it very clear that He came to serve, not be served (Matthew 20:28). He was so committed to service that just hours before His death we find Him performing one of His last and most humble acts of service, that of washing His disciples' feet. Given that He knew what lay ahead for Him—that His last act of service would be the ordeal of the cross—it would have been understandable if He had lingered at the table and allowed the disciples to minister to Him. Instead, He got down on His hands and knees in order to serve them. I am amazed every time I think of the fact that the Son of God, who rightfully deserved to be served, modeled for us the importance of filling our lives with service instead.

Service matters to God. When God chose a mother for His only son, He chose Mary, in part because she evidenced a servant's heart (Luke 1:38). In the book of Revelation, Jesus commends the church in Thyatira for "deeds" and "service" (Revelation 2:19 NASB). Service is so important to God that over and over in Scripture we are told that it is one of the things that He will reward. Ephesians 6:7-8 (NIV) encourages: "Serve wholeheartedly, as if you were serving the Lord, not people, because you know that the Lord will reward each one for whatever good they do...."

Service is not cheap and it is seldom easy. The commitment to serve others will always cost us something. It cost Christ everything, and while it is doubtful that it will cost any of us as much, genuine service will require sacrifice. In the parable of the Good Samaritan, it cost the Samaritan plenty to be of service to the battered man lying in the road. He, like all the others who had passed by the man that day, needed to be somewhere, so stopping to dress his wounds cost him time and an extra day on the road; putting the man on his own donkey required that he walk, which cost him energy; and paying for him to stay in a hotel cost him two silver coins. But because he had compassion on the man, he was willing to serve. Jesus referred to his act of service as simply being neighborly (Luke 10:25-37).

Too often when it comes to service, we are more like the man to whom Jesus directed this parable, rather than the Samaritan. Scripture indicates that the man who asked Jesus to define the concept of *neighbor* was attempting to "justify his actions." We are like this man whenever we rationalize our failure to serve by using lack of time, energy, or money as an excuse. The reality is that service is not optional for those of us who are serious about living the truths of both Scripture and the Serenity Prayer. Jesus once commented to His disciples that "the workers are few" (Matthew 9:37). Unfortunately that fact, which was true in His lifetime, continues to be relevant today. The world is still lacking in unselfish people committed to service. As Christians we sell the concept of giving to God short when we think in terms of monetary giving only. While God certainly deserves our tithes and offerings, money is no obstacle for God. God needs people, not money, because it is through people that His grace is administered. Successfully practicing "not as

I would have it" requires that we recognize the daily opportunities He places in our life to act in gracious, unselfish ways. Achieving this unselfish ambition requires an ongoing, sustained commitment to willing service which moves us away from preoccupation with self and into the needs of an empty, hurting world.

I once saw a bumper sticker that read, "Practice random acts of kindness." At the time I thought it was a nice sentiment and that the world would probably be a better place if everyone took this idea to heart. After practicing the principles of the Serenity Prayer for many years, it occurred to me that this seemingly nice sentiment was part of my problem all along. I *was* practicing random acts of kindness. They were random in that I performed them when I felt like it, or when I was particularly moved by a need, or when there was something to be gained, like recognition or approval. Those "kind" acts were selfish as well as random. I now realize that living serenity requires that I be committed to *willful* acts of service which steer me away from selfishness and toward deliberate attempts to make this sinful world a slightly better place.

"Not as I Would Have It" and Me

I owe my serenity to the Serenity Prayer, but I owe my sobriety to service. In fact, I do not think that it is an overstatement to say that I owe my life to service. Had I not become involved in service, I undoubtedly would have returned to the walking death of my addiction. Service to others was the prescription that helped to change my innate struggle with selfishness.

Of course, before recovery I didn't consider myself to be selfish. Early in our marriage in the heat of an argument, my husband called me selfish. The idea that I was selfish was so repulsive to me that it felt as though I had been slapped in the face. How could he possibly say that? I was the epitome of a giving, selfless person. Unfortunately, being under the influence of my untreated codependency at the time, I mistook my resentment-laced, obligation-inspired "giving" as service and my lack of identity as unselfishness. I didn't realize that denying self and not having a self were two completely different things. It took the principles of the Serenity Prayer to bring me face-to-face with the true nature of my selfish condition, and it took service to others to move me away from it.

The commitment to service that I made early in my recovery kept me coming back to my recovery group week after week. There were nights when I had other places I would rather have been and other things that I would have rather been doing, but because people were counting on me and the duties I needed to perform, I showed up. Eventually, performing service helped me to stay connected to the group long enough to learn the value of group attendance. When I was in a terrible place, I needed the group. And when I was in an especially good place, the group needed me. So regardless of which emotional state I happened to be in, there was no reasonable excuse for failing to attend my group.

As I followed through on my commitment to service, I was amazed at the blessings I received. It is a scriptural principle that when we give, we receive more than we give away. Jesus said, "Give, and you will receive. Your gift will return to you in full—pressed down, shaken together to make room for more, running over, and poured into your lap. The amount you give will determine the amount you get back" (Luke 6:38). Through willing service, I have found that the promise contained in Christ's words never fails to materialize. The more I give, the more I receive. Most of the time it is not a monetary blessing that I receive, but instead the sense of well-being and serenity that follows an act of service. I am aware of it as I drive home from the meeting in which I served, or when I hang up the phone after taking a phone call from someone who is struggling, or after praying with someone I sponsor. The benefits of service are priceless.

Fortunately, there are no acts of service that are considered too small in God's estimation. Jesus said that if I give even a cup of water in His name, it is an act of service (Mark 9:41). What a relief to know that because all acts of service to others are ultimately service to God, even the seemingly minor, insignificant things I do, when done in a spirit of humility and compassion, matter to Him. This puts the simple act of making coffee at my recovery group in a whole new light. While I have always believed in the importance of tithing to God, through service I have come to realize how important it is to tithe both my time and talents and not simply my money. In fact, sometimes it is actually easier to give money rather than time or talents. Yet any talent or ability that I possess was given to me by God for the purpose of serving others.

Years into my recovery, I continue to struggle with selfishness. It rears its ugly head in one form or another every single day. I have to fight the urge to put myself on the top rung of the ladder, and instead humbly descend into the circle of fellowship through service. I have no doubt that I will need to diligently practice the principle of "not as I would have it" for the rest of my life. But it is certainly worth the effort.

Because in light of all that God has done for me, giving back through service seems like a small thing—a most reasonable response to His amazing grace. And so I give in gratitude, in serenity, and in the hope that I will continue in His service every day of my life.

"Not as I Would Have It" and You

1. How do you display selfishness in your life?

2. How do you display greed in your life?

3. How do you display self-indulgence in your life?

4. How do you display selfish ambition in your life?

5. Has selfish ambition ever affected your relationships? If so, in what way?

6. Do you treat yourself with the same level of regard that you treat others?

7. How are you using your time and talents in the service of others?

8. What warning does Scripture give regarding greed, pride, and selfishness? (Ezekiel 33:31; Matthew 6:19-21; Mark 10:23; Luke 12:15-21; Luke 16:13; Romans 7:8; Galatians 6:7-8; Galatians 6:14; Philippians 2:3-4)

9. What do the following Scriptures reveal regarding the consequences of pride and/or greed? Which have you experienced? (2 Chronicles 33:23; Psalm 18:27; Proverbs 13:10; Proverbs 16:18; Proverbs 29:23; Isaiah 2:11, 17; Isaiah 13:11; Isaiah 26:5-6; Daniel 5:19-21)

10. What do the following Scriptures identify as the benefits of humility? How has exercising humility benefitted your recovery? (Deuteronomy 8:2; Psalm 37:11; Isaiah 29:19; Micah 6:8; Matthew 18:4; Matthew 23:12)

11. What do the following Scriptures reveal regarding God's response to humility? (1 Samuel 2:7-8; 1 Kings 21:29; 2 Chronicles 33:12-13; Psalm 25:9; Psalm 147:6; Psalm 149:4; Isaiah 66:2; Daniel 10:12; James 4:6, 10)

12. What instructions do the following Scriptures give regarding service? (Matthew 5:16; Matthew 6:1; Mark 10:42-45; Luke 6:38; John 13:13-17; 2 Corinthians 8:7; 2 Corinthians 9:6-7; Galatians 6:7-10; 1 Peter 4:10)

13. What do the following Scriptures indicate regarding how we are to serve each other? Which of these are you doing? (Romans 12:10, 13, 16, 20; Romans 14:13, 19; Galatians 6:2; Ephesians 4:2, 32; Hebrews 13:16; James 5:16; 1 Peter 3:8; 1 Peter 4:8-9; 1 Peter 5:5-6)

14. What idea from this chapter do you plan to put into practice?

Chapter Fifteen: Trusting

It is probably safe to say that most of us who find ourselves in a twelve-step program have issues with trust. Because the inability to trust can have such a painful impact on our lives, many of us have used a variety of addictive processes as a form of pain management. We thought we were just helping ourselves manage the pitfalls of life. It probably never occurred to us that there was a trust issue at the core of our compulsive behaviors. But according to the Serenity Prayer, we will be unable to experience serenity unless we learn to trust again.

The ability to trust plays a critical role in human development. It is the primary developmental task humans confront during the first year of life. In order to develop a sense of trust, it is imperative that an infant experience certain conditions within their relationships with significant others as well as the environment. These conditions include having basic needs for food and safety met, as well as adequate nurturing from significant others. If these needs are met in a timely and consistent manner, then the outcome will be a state of trust and security. The infant will learn that the world is predictable and safe and that people can be depended upon. On the other hand, if the infant is met with deprivation, inconsistency, and indifference, then the result will be a state of mistrust. Because each of the various developmental stages we pass through over the course of our lifetime builds on the previous stage, failure to develop trust can have far-reaching, detrimental effects on personality development and maturity.

While situations which compromise the experience of trust can occur during any stage of psychosocial development, those that occur earlier in life have the capacity to produce effects which are more damaging and pervasive than those that occur later in life. These effects become emotional handicaps which can be difficult to overcome. Growing up in a family where there is active, untreated addiction can impair a child's development of trust. This stems from inconsistencies in parenting exhibited by an addicted parent. A parent who is incapacitated by an addiction will be unable to provide the basic level of care needed by the child in a consistent manner. Mood swings, which often accompany addiction, can add an element of unpredictability to the environment. It is important to remember that it is not just the addicted parent whose parenting abilities are compromised. Spouses can be distracted, distressed, and emotionally unavailable to their children as a result of ongoing exposure to the disease of untreated addiction in the other parent. Additionally, research has documented that children living with substance-abusing parents are more likely to experience physical abuse, making the home a dangerous rather than safe place.[38] Within an addictive environment, trust and mistrust are continually doing battle.

While injuries to trust that occur later in life may not carry as pervasive effects on development as those occurring while trust is being formed, on an emotional level they can be just as painful and damaging. In adulthood, there are a number of ways that our ability to trust others can be compromised. We need to be able to take people at their word, and when they break their promises or fail to tell the truth, our ability to trust them is diminished. We need to believe that those we trust have our best interests in mind, and when they take advantage of us instead, it reduces our level of trust. Trust requires openness, honesty, and respect to thrive; deception, exploitation, and selfishness will eventually extinguish it.

Another situation that has damaging effects on the ability to trust is abandonment. Regardless of whether it occurs in childhood or adulthood, abandonment is one of the single most painful experiences people created by God for intimate fellowship with each other can experience. Jesus endured mocking, flogging, beating, and humiliation prior to arriving at the cross. Yet it was the pain of abandonment that caused Him to cry out those anguished words, "My

God, my God, why have You abandoned me?" (Matthew 27:46). His choice to save humankind by taking on the sin of the world resulted in separation from a perfect God. This sense of abandonment from the Father He so loved was unbearable. The next time He cried out from the cross it was to place His Spirit in the hands of His Father, thereby regaining through death and resurrection the intimacy of their relationship.

Abandonment may visit us in many different forms. Sometimes abandonment is unintentional, such as when a parent dies or is hospitalized or unable to perform their parental responsibilities due to prolonged or chronic illness. Abandonment can come in the form of extensive absences due to job travel, the need to work multiple jobs, or lengthy work days. At other times abandonment occurs in the form of infidelity or divorce. The distrust which results from the experience of abandonment has the potential to impair future relationships. Fear of abandonment can leave us reluctant to risk the possibility of that degree of pain again by allowing people to get "too close." Trust becomes replaced by fear, and in our need to protect ourselves we erect walls to guard against vulnerability. Those walls, which initially begin as a form of pain management, ultimately wall in our pain.

Unfortunately, we were never intended to live life from behind a wall of fear and isolation. Life behind the wall may offer the illusion of security and protection, but mostly it is just lonely, and that loneliness brings a pain of its own. Behind the wall, disconnected and alone, we have no hope of learning to trust again. What we truly need when we are hurting is sanctuary in the form of divine refuge, rather than self-imposed exile behind walls of isolation.

If our inability to trust affected just our social and interpersonal relationships, that alone would be enough to disrupt our ability to experience serenity. Regrettably, it impacts us on a spiritual level also, as the lack of trust which originated from our human relationships can become projected into our relationship with God. When this happens, serenity becomes impossible because we are unable to do what the prayer encourages us to do. The prayer says "trusting," which implies that we are to live in a continual state of trust in God. An ongoing experience of serenity is derived from the enduring certainty that God is who He says He is and will do what He says He will do.

Scripture confirms that trusting God is the path to lasting serenity. Isaiah 26:3 says that God keeps us in "perfect peace," in other words an abiding state of serenity, when we place ongoing trust in Him. The idea that serenity is a by-product of trusting God is reinforced by Romans 15:13 (NIV), which says, "May the God of hope fill you with all joy and peace as you trust in him, so that you may overflow with hope by the power of the Holy Spirit." It is while we exercise trust in God that we experience serenity. One of the last pieces of advice that Jesus gave to His disciples concerned the importance of well-placed trust: "Don't let your hearts be troubled. Trust in God, and trust also in me" (John 14:1). The only appropriate solution to fear is to trust God and to say as David said, "When I am afraid, I will put my trust in you" (Psalm 56:3 NASB).

Proverbs 3:5 encourages the cautious person to "trust in the Lord with all your heart." When we make the decision to wholeheartedly trust God, we have so much to gain and so little, besides our fear, to lose. The many benefits that trusting God imparts are described in Jeremiah 17:7-8, which says, "But blessed are those who trust in the Lord and have made the Lord their hope and confidence. They are like trees planted along a riverbank, with roots that reach deep into the water. Such trees are not bothered by the heat or worried by long months of drought. Their leaves stay green, and they never stop producing fruit." Trusting God forms the secure foundation from which we can face the insecurity of life. It keeps us rooted and growing. We can stand "the heat"; in other words, we can handle any adverse conditions that come our way and flourish instead of worry. Yet above all this we are told that the ultimate benefit of trusting God is that we are guaranteed to produce fruit, which means develop character. For recovering people who are seeking to have our character defects replaced by the character of Christ, this is indeed good news.

God can be trusted because He exhibits trustworthy character. There are several characteristics which constitute trustworthiness such as truthfulness, consistency, dependability, and safety. Scripture reveals that all of these are part of God's character. God is so truthful that in the book of Isaiah He is called the "God of truth"—it is simply part of His identity (Isaiah 65:16). He is so consistent that He says of Himself, "I am the Lord, and I do not change" (Malachi 3:6). He is so dependable that He doesn't just make promises—He makes everlasting covenants that cannot be broken (Genesis 9:16). Because He is a fortress, shield, stronghold, and refuge (Psalm 18:2; Nahum 1:7), we can stop building walls of protection and instead find safety and shelter in Him. While these characteristics may have been missing from our earthly relationships, God does not fail to bring them into His.

God values trust. He longs for people to trust Him. The Old Testament records story upon story of His miraculous provision and protection intended to inspire trust in the people He loved. The New Testament reveals that faith, which is a form of trust, was the only thing that ever impressed Jesus. He never extolled the rich for their wealth or the powerful for their success, but He did commend people who evidenced great faith; it both amazed and astonished Him (Luke 7:9; Matthew 8:10).

How sad it is to realize that I often fail to trust God, the only Being who is infallibly trustworthy, simply on the basis of my past distrustful experiences with people. When I stop to ponder this, it lacks logic. After all, God can't take advantage of me or use me, because he doesn't need anything from me; He has everything (Job 22:2). God doesn't play favorites, so I am assured that I matter to Him just as much as anyone else; He's not going to replace me (Ephesians 6:9). He finishes what He begins, so He isn't going to give up on me (Philippians 1:6). God can never lie to me because the Bible is clear that God is incapable of lying—it doesn't exist in His character (Hebrews 6:18). God always keeps His promises; He has to—His reputation is at stake. Scripture records many times that when God fulfilled His promises, it was "for the sake of His great name" (1 Samuel 12:22 NIV). The Bible records hundreds of His promises, and one of these is that He will never forsake or abandon me (Hebrews 13:5). He describes His commitment to me by saying: "Can a mother forget her nursing child? Can she feel no love for a child she has borne? But even if that were possible, I would not forget you!" (Isaiah 49:15). These are comforting words to a cautious, insecure waif like me.

While God is completely trustworthy, the same cannot be said for all people. As I have practiced the principles of the Serenity Prayer and my serenity has grown, I have come to the realization that the challenge for me today is not so much an inability to trust as it is misplaced trust. At this point in my recovery, the question is not whether I am capable of trusting others; the question is whether I am capable of recognizing trustworthy people. When we naïvely put our trust in people who are not trustworthy, we will inevitably experience disappointment and pain.

Scripture encourages us to trust God and love people. Sometimes we get this admonition reversed and instead love God and put our trust in people. At other times we fail to distinguish between loving people and trusting people, which can be problematic because the two are not one and the same. Some of the people we love are not necessarily worthy of our trust. Scripture clearly encourages us to love others. In fact, we are even encouraged to love our enemies (Matthew 5:44); however we aren't encouraged to trust them! It is entirely possible to earnestly love someone without trusting them—just ask any parent of an addict.

One of the life skills that recovering people need to learn is the ability to evaluate who is trustworthy and who is unreliable, who is safe and who is harmful. Proverbs 18:24 tells us that "a real friend sticks closer than a brother." Because practicing openness and honesty is vital to recovery as well as the development of trust, it is just that "sticky" kind of friend we need to find. Learning who can be trusted will require willingness to risk as well as patience. A key element in the development of trusting relationships is consistency with regard to truthfulness, thoughtfulness, and reliability. Because consistency of character can only be proven over time, learning to trust will require an investment of time without a guaranteed outcome, and therefore contains an element of risk. If we are serious about correcting misplaced trust, then we will need to resist the urge to rush into "trusting" relationships.

While we sometimes misplace our trust by putting it in people who are incapable of delivering, we just as often misplace it by expecting from them what can only come through God. Some of these unrealistic expectations include perfect love, unconditional acceptance, and future security. Isaiah 2:22 warns: "Don't put your trust in mere humans. They are as frail as breath." Our quest for serenity is much better served by placing our trust in God first and people second.

It is comforting to realize that even people lauded for their faith shared the same struggles with trusting God that the rest of us have experienced. Thankfully, God didn't exclude these stories from His Word. While the accounts of their victories give hope for the future, it is reading about their struggles with faith that reassure and encourage us. Stories like that of Hezekiah, who, in spite of having been assured by God that he would be healed, asked for a sign to confirm it (2 Kings 20:1-11). Or Gideon, who laid out a fleece and received a clear answer from God, but needed to do it a second time just to make sure he hadn't misjudged the results (Judges 6:36-40). Because these illustrations are so like my own fluctuating level of trust, it is heartening to realize that God's response was to simply recognize the frailty of human trust and provide the needed reassurance.

Fortunately, the "trusting" referred to in the Serenity Prayer is an ongoing process. I don't need inordinate amounts of trust in order to practice this principle. Jesus said that trust (or faith) the size of a mustard seed was all that was needed to get started (Matthew 17:20). I can learn to trust God more and more, one moment at a time, and as I do so, my trust will grow into the kind of trust I truly desire—trust like David's as he went out to meet Goliath. I can just imagine the young teenager dressed in King Saul's oversized armor. What a sight that must have been—all that heavy metal dragging on the ground, the bronze helmet painfully weighing down his head. David may have heard the mocking of the Philistine army and realized what a ridiculous sight he was, but that was not why he shed that heavy armor.

It was his trust in God that inspired him to take it off. David realized that a coat of armor and a sword were simply things, and things could not be trusted to save. He was used to counting on God alone in difficult situations. Past experiences with wild animal attacks had convinced him that God could be counted on to give him all the ability he needed to subdue even a giant and so there was no reason to be afraid (1 Samuel 17:38-50). Over the course of his lifetime, David would experience betrayal by a wife, a father-in-law, children, military advisors, and close friends; yet in spite of this, by focusing on God's trustworthiness he arrived at the end of his life sure of God's unchanging promises, secure in His salvation, and serenely convinced that his trust had been well placed (2 Samuel 23:5).

I once heard a military survival expert say that faith in God was one of the most important factors in predicting survival abilities in extreme situations. If trusting God is so beneficial in the extreme cases like David's, it is certainly sufficient to banish my common ordinary fear, leaving both security and serenity in its place.

Deborah Galasso

"Trusting" and Me

I will never forget the moment when I accidentally uncovered the most serious core issue hampering my ability to experience serenity. I was attending an educational conference on addiction and recovery at the time. The speaker had said something to the effect of: "Life is like a free fall, and all of us are screaming on the way down. Some of us are screaming in sheer terror because we have no idea where we will land. And others of us are screaming in exhilaration because we know that when we get to the end of the fall, the loving hands of God will be there to catch us." As I sat in that room with hundreds of other people, tears began to well up in my eyes and spill down my cheeks, much to my embarrassment. Those tears were the result of an overwhelming sadness that swept over me, like a wave crashing on a sea shore, as I suddenly realized that I was one of those people screaming in terror. And if the analogy given by the speaker were true, then it was because I didn't believe that God would catch me. I was not trusting God to be there for me.

Up to that point in my recovery, I thought that my primary core issue was fear, when in reality it was lack of trust. Every fear I had experienced in the past and all of those that I would confront in the future had one thing in common: they were rooted in lack of faith in God. In all the months I had spent in therapy I had been asking the wrong question. The question was not: could I stop being afraid? The question was: could I trust God enough? It was evident that in order to experience the serenity promised by the Serenity Prayer, I would first need to address my lack of trust in God.

The truth was that I was not a very trusting person in general. I had a tendency to be aloof with people and somewhat suspicious of their motives. This was partly a function of my previous experiences with abandonment and partly a function of my low self-esteem. The problem was not simply that I didn't trust people—I didn't trust myself either. I had made many unwise decisions which had landed me in some deep, dark holes. Experiencing serenity would require that I learn to trust myself as well as God and others.

For no logical reason, the greatest fear in my life was that of financial insecurity. In spite of a stable, well-paying job, I somehow frightened myself into believing that destitution was lurking somewhere on the horizon, and with it the possibility that I could end up living my life out of a shopping cart. As I recall this now, it seems ludicrous to me. But I guess that is why fear has been referred to as "false evidence appearing real." The turning point in my journey of learning to trust came when I ran across what I now like to refer to as the "bag lady Scripture." It was penned by David and is found in Psalm 37:25: "Once I was young, and now I am old. Yet I have never seen the godly abandoned, or their children begging for bread."

Because of that Scripture, I made a conscious decision that no matter what happened in my life, I was going to practice the principle of trusting God first and foremost. There was no shortage of opportunities to put that decision into practice. One such opportunity occurred when we had to place my mother in a nursing home. The decision to do so was difficult because of our concern about the quality of care that she would receive. Had I not trusted that God cared about her welfare even more than I did and that He had the ability to provide her with everything she needed in my absence, it would have been impossible to walk out of that nursing home without her. True to His promises, He provided her with a wonderful Christian nurse, who lovingly cared for her until the end of her life.

When we were confronted with legal issues, I reminded myself that my trust was in God, not lawyers and judges. When my trust wavered the day before court, I called my aunt to pray for me. She prayed that God would give the judge a "new set of eyes" with which to view the case. God did better than that. When we went to court the next day, a whole new judge had been assigned to our case.

Another time I had an interaction with a sponsor which left me feeling angry and misunderstood. When I am hurting, my instinct is to run from people first and ask questions later. While I struggled with the question of whether or not I could or should trust her, I decided to place my trust in the God of reconciliation instead, and believe that He would guide me through my bruised feelings and confused thoughts. It took many months, but eventually God put me in situations which revealed my errors in perception, and I was able to make amends and reconcile with her.

One day I was disturbed to realize that although I believed that God was faithful and worthy of my trust, when confronted with a problem I would often find myself saying, "I'll just have to trust God with that." On the one hand, it was just a harmless expression, but on the other hand, I recognized the falsehood contained in that simple statement. The truth is that I don't *have to* trust God—it is a free will choice I make moment by moment. To say that I "have to trust God," makes it sound as if it is some desperate last resort—as though I've tried everything else, so now "I'll just have to trust Him." Because I in no way wish to demean God's remarkable faithfulness to me, I have decided to replace that expression with this truth: "I am choosing to trust God."

There aren't many things that derail my serenity these days, especially not the fear of becoming a "bag lady." As I survey the course of my life, I can confidently confirm what David expressed so long ago: I was once young and now I am old, yet God has never failed me. His faithfulness has caused my trust to so greatly increase that at this point in my recovery, even if I were to become a "bag lady," I would trust God to provide me with the best shopping cart in the parking lot to serenely push along as we continued our journey together.

"Trusting" and You

1. What experiences in your past have affected your ability to trust?

____
____
____
____
____
____

2. Would you describe yourself as overly trusting or too distrustful? What problems has this caused for you?

____
____
____
____

3. What characteristics of God's trustworthiness have you experienced in your recovery?

____
____
____
____

4. What are some situations in which you have chosen to trust God and what were the outcomes?

____
____
____
____

5. How are you working on building trusting relationships in your life? With whom can you be open and honest?

____
____
____
____

6. Are there people in your life who are not trustworthy? How can you show love in the absence of trust?

____
____
____
____

7. How has your ability to evaluate safe versus harmful relationships improved over the course of your recovery? How can you continue to work on this area?

____
____
____
____

8. What do the following Scriptures reveal about why God can be trusted? Which of these attributes are most important to you? (Numbers 23:19; Joshua 23:14; 2 Chronicles 19:7; Psalm 33:4; Psalm 100:5; Psalm 102:27; Psalm 111:7-8; Psalm 139:7-12; Isaiah 45:19; 2 Timothy 2:13; 2 Timothy 4:16-17; Hebrews 6:17-18)

____
____
____
____
____
____
____
____

9. What do the following Scriptures identify as the benefits of trusting God? (2 Kings 18:5-7; Psalm 4:8; Psalm 22:4-5; Psalm 25:3; Psalm 52:8; Psalm 112:7; Psalm 125:1; Proverbs 28:25-26; Isaiah 25:9)

____
____
____
____
____
____

10. What warnings do the following Scriptures give about trusting others? (Psalm 40:4; Psalm 118:8-9; Psalm 146:3; Proverbs 12:26; Jeremiah 7:8; Jeremiah 9:4-6; Jeremiah 17:5; Micah 7:5-6; Matthew 7:15-20)

11. What do the following Scriptures suggest about trusting things? (Psalm 20:7-8; Psalm 44:6-8; Psalm 62:10)

12. What do the following Scriptures teach about God's promises? (Deuteronomy 4:31; Deuteronomy 7:9; 2 Samuel 7:28; 1 Kings 8:56; Psalm 119:50, 89; Psalm 145:13; Jeremiah 32:40-41; Jeremiah 33:19-21; 1 Peter 1:25)

13. What do the following Scriptures disclose about God's reputation? (1 Samuel 12:22; Psalm 106:8; Ezekiel 20:9, 14, 22, 44; Ezekiel 36:22)

14. What idea from this chapter do you plan to put into practice?

Chapter Sixteen: That You Will Make All Things Right

In my quest for living serenity, I am learning the importance of understanding the difference between my job description and God's. His job is to "make all things right," and my job is to trust that He will. Too often I find myself attempting to force "right" solutions and achieve certain outcomes which, according to the Serenity Prayer, is not my responsibility. It happens on such a regular basis that it just seems to be my natural inclination. Despite my concerted efforts, before I know it I have slipped into trying to do God's job for Him. I am not so grandiose as to actually think that I can perform His job; yet my desire to have things go a certain way and my actions directed toward that end suggest otherwise. Whenever I begin to stray away from managing my job into attempting to take over God's, I am left with feelings of frustration and failure rather than serenity, the outcome I desire.

God is qualified for the job of making "all things right" because He is the God of all things. Romans 11:36 (NASB) says: "For from Him and through Him and to Him are all things." Paul said that there is "one God and Father, who is over all and in all and living through all" (Ephesians 4:6). He can accomplish things within me and through me and around me that I cannot. He can make "all things right" because "He existed before anything else, and he holds all creation together" (Colossians 1:17). While I may, at times, feel as though things in my life are unmanageable and falling apart, God has them securely within His grasp. Paul went on to say that God had reconciled all things to Himself by providing a once and for all solution for the problem of sin (Colossians 1:20). God can make "all things right" in my journey of recovery because He is an expert at making things that are in opposition to each other compatible and acceptable.

The challenge in attempting to live out this portion of the prayer is to remember that my perception of "all things right" may differ from God's. Because He is the God of all, God is concerned with *all* things, whereas I am usually concerned with only *some* things. While I am interested in God intervening in certain unmanageable aspects of my life, God is interested in my whole life, not simply certain parts. Wholeness involves every facet of my being—spiritual, emotional, mental, social, and physical. Scripture records the story of Jesus encountering a man who had been an invalid for thirty-eight years. His question to the man was: "Wilt thou be made whole?" (John 5:6 KJV). It is interesting that His question was not: "Do you want to walk?" The answer to that would have been pretty obvious. Jesus was concerned about the man's wholeness, not simply his disability. And that's the way God works. He is not content to work on just the obvious, like my addiction, but instead goes to work on the subtle areas that need to be made right also.

God's desire to make "all things right" means He is concerned with everyone, not just me. Romans 8:28 indicates that "God causes everything to work together for the good of those who love God...." God wants all things to be right for everyone. That means that at the point at which my life intersects with someone else's, He is not just thinking about what would be good for me; He is considering what is good for the other person too. It helps me to maintain my sense of serenity when I remember that because my life is so intricately interwoven into the lives of others, it may sometimes seem that the things that are working for good in someone else's life are bringing discomfort to mine. For example, when an alcoholic hits bottom it is a painful time for the whole family, yet this is often the circumstance that leads the codependent, who thinks they do not have a problem, into treatment. God can use the process of an alcoholic hitting bottom to eventually make all things right in not only the life of the alcoholic, but those affected by their disease as well. A dear friend in recovery often reminds me that it was the pain of her husband's addiction that ultimately motivated her to seek help through a twelve-step group and find the serenity that she would not otherwise have known.

To the detriment of my serenity, I sometimes delude myself into thinking that "all things right" means that I will find myself in pleasing circumstances. However, because God is more concerned with my character development than my comfort, He would rather change me from within than simply alter my external circumstances. That is because God is able to take the worst of circumstances and cause good to result from them.

Consider the story of Joseph, who had the grave misfortune of being the first case of human trafficking recorded in Scripture. He was sold into slavery by his jealous brothers and taken to Egypt (Genesis 37:12-36). This was an extremely bad circumstance, but God allowed him to end up working for one of Pharaoh's officials, which was not so bad. However, after doing the right thing and resisting the overtures of his master's wife, Joseph was falsely accused of rape and ended up in prison. This was an extremely bad circumstance, yet God gave him favor with the warden so that he was not only put in charge of other prisoners, but also received catered food rather than the usual prison fare. Ultimately Pharaoh had a troubling dream that could not be interpreted by his advisors and because Joseph was known around the prison for his ability to interpret dreams, he got the gig. Pharaoh was so impressed with Joseph that he made him one of his top advisors, and it was Joseph's God-inspired advice that saved Egypt from starvation and ultimately reunited him with his Hebrew family and saved them from starvation. Joseph's final analysis of his unfortunate circumstances is found in Genesis 50:20: "You intended to harm me, but God intended it all for good. He brought me to this position so I could save the lives of many people."

Often it is only with the perspective of time that we are able to see that God has redeemed a bad circumstance in our life and made it right. It may be years or decades before His restorative work is realized. When Adam and Eve sinned, causing the fall of humankind, God promised that He would make all things right once again (Genesis 3:15); yet it would be centuries before Christ's work on the cross fulfilled this promise.

In reference to God's promised redemption, Paul said, "When we were utterly helpless, Christ came at just the right time and died for us sinners" (Romans 5:6). Whenever I read this Scripture, I cannot help but wonder: wouldn't any point in time at which Christ died have fulfilled God's promise? After all, we would have been completely powerless to save ourselves no matter what century it was. But God had "just the right time" in mind and so Christ's death coincided with the Passover and He became "the Lamb of God who takes away the sin of the world" (John 1:29), which reminds me that God's timing is much more infinitely precise and purposeful than my own.

King Solomon said that people cannot comprehend the extent of what God has done from beginning to end (Ecclesiastes 3:11). Because He sees past, present, and future, He is aware of things I cannot see and He knows things that I cannot know—such as when my heart is ready for change and can make the most of an opportunity for growth, or when it would instead be crushed or hardened by an experience coming too soon. Because He sees the end as well as the beginning, He is aware of untoward consequences that I may not consider. While it may have seemed like a good idea to the Israelites to move quickly into the Promised Land—after all, it was promised to them— God told Moses that the reason for driving the occupying nations out a little at a time rather than all at once was to prevent the land from becoming desolate and overrun by wild animals (Exodus 23:29). Given my impulsive tendencies, I am a lot like the children of Israel and prefer the all at once approach, blithely unaware that the consequences of such dramatic change may, in the end, actually lead me away from serenity. My job is to learn to trust that God has good reasons for working in my life little by little, day by day, one moment at a time.

Sometimes I am so focused on trying to understand how God is executing His job that I forfeit my serenity. My attempts to "figure God out" usually go something like this: "*Why* is this happening? Why *isn't* this happening? Why *now*? Why *not* now? *How* can He possibly make this right? *When* will He make it right?" In other words, I am basically spinning my wheels on questions that cannot be answered by me. There are many things in this world that I do not understand and cannot explain. The eleventh chapter of Hebrews tells us that many of the "faith hall of famers" didn't see the outcomes they were expecting during their lifetime, but they continued to trust God anyway. Overanalyzing is seldom productive and does little to move me closer to God's peace, which is far more wonderful than the human mind can understand (Philippians 4:7). God has at His disposal an unlimited number of ways to make all things right that I cannot begin to comprehend. If I truly desire serenity, I must resist the urge to ruminate about the "How?" and "Why?"

Paul reminded us that because God's infinite power is at work within us, He is able to accomplish results that we cannot possibly achieve or even imagine (Ephesians 3:20). God has unlimited ways and means of making all things right for us, regardless of negative circumstances or impossible situations. Because He works on the inside, He is able to work with hearts and minds. One way that He accomplishes this inner work is through divine revelation, such as He did for Hagar after she was sent away by Abraham. It was not until God opened her eyes that Hagar, despairing of life and dying of thirst, was able to see the well of water there in the desert (Genesis 21:14-19). The well of water was there the entire time she was wandering, but given her despondent state of mind she was unable to see it. Just as in Hagar's case, sometimes the solution can be starring us in the face, yet until God brings clarity and revelation we are unable to see it. Because addiction is a disease of denial, and denial is a form of being unwilling to see, we will repeatedly need God to bring things to light in order to make all things right.

Often it is through Scripture that God brings revelation and makes all things right within us. What we read in Scripture may cause us to change our perception about a difficult circumstance. Sometimes He makes all things right by using His Word to prepare us for a circumstance that lies ahead. A friend told me of a time that God impressed her to carefully consider a certain passage of Scripture during a Sunday sermon. She wrote the reference down, looked it up when she returned home, and found that it spoke of God's ability to sustain and guide. While she thought that it was a wonderful and hopeful promise, at that point in time it did not hold particular significance for her. But within a matter of weeks she was suddenly and dramatically thrust into a situation of betrayal so painful that it was only by standing on that Scripture that she could face each stressful, uncertain day.

At other times God makes all things right by providing resources that we are lacking so that we are sustained during bad circumstances. These resources may include, among other things, information, money, or people. I remember when I was experiencing insomnia during the initial weeks of abstinence. I was mindlessly channel surfing in the middle of the night when I ran across a program discussing herbal supplements. The health practitioner just happened to be talking about herbs that were effective in alleviating insomnia and anxiety. The next day I obtained one of them and it helped greatly. Given that one of the most common reasons people return to their addiction is due to withdrawal symptoms, that herbal supplement had far more important consequences than simply providing a good night's sleep, reminding me once again that God's sweeping objective is to make *all* things right.

People are another resource God provides to help make all things right within us. Paul often made reference in his letters to the vital role other Christians played in helping to sustain him during trying times in his ministry. Many times he noted the ability of godly people to "refresh" each other's spirits (1 Corinthians 16:18; 2 Corinthians 7:13 NASB). In particular, Paul credited the prayers of others as being an important conduit of hope and support, once declaring, "For I know that as you pray for me and the Spirit of Jesus Christ helps me, this will lead to my deliverance" (Philippians 1:19). This declaration in the belief that God would make all things right is even more meaningful when we realize that Paul said this while still in chains. It just goes to show the refreshing effect those prayers were having on his spirit! Providing people who will pray for us is a way that God sustains us while in difficult circumstances. Although my own prayers are an effective channel of spiritual sustenance while waiting for God to "make all things right," in order to feel "all right" in the mean time, it helps to know that others are praying for me. And what is even more refreshing to my spirit than simply *knowing* that someone is praying for me is actually *hearing* someone pray for me.

Often God makes us "all right" in our circumstances by bringing comfort during trying times. The methods He uses to accomplish this are varied and highly personal: a thank you card arriving in the mail on a particularly discouraging day; a reading from a daily devotional which addresses a particular aspect of our struggle; an encouraging phone call or email when plagued by self-doubt. While these things are encouraging in and of themselves, more importantly they remind us that God is not just aware of our distress but concerned by it as well. Because of His compassionate nature, He will go to great lengths to comfort us as we walk through the painful circumstances of life.

Bob, a close friend of mine, suffered incapacitating grief following the death of his mother. Although his mother was a devout Christian, and he believed in heaven and eternal live, he found himself crying inconsolably and struggling with depression. This continued for a period of time in spite of the prayers and encouragement he received from his family and friends. Finally one night he had a dream in which he received a phone call from his mother. She told him that she was calling him from heaven where she was alive and well, and that she didn't want him to worry about her anymore. The dream was so vivid, and his recall of the details so complete, that he was convinced it was a message from God. From that moment on he didn't experience depression again.

God knows exactly what will bring comfort, and over the years I have heard a wide variety of ways God has orchestrated uniquely personal grief counseling: a rainbow that appears at the funeral of a young child who had a passion for drawing colorful rainbows; a hummingbird hovers above the eulogizer at the funeral of a beloved mother, bringing comfort to her distraught daughter; a swarm of dragonflies appear in the garden of a woman who has just lost her best friend who happened to be an avid gardener. While the appearance of a hummingbird probably wouldn't have resonated with my friend Bob, a vivid dream certainly did. Whether in the form of dreams, rainbows, or flying creatures, God understands just what symbolism will cut through the intensity of our suffering and quiet our hurting hearts, thereby enabling us to be "all right" in even the most painful of circumstances.

One of the most challenging areas in which to apply this principle of allowing God to make "all things right" is when we believe we have been wronged. When we are hurt, it is tempting to want to right the situation in our own way, rather than wait for God to make it right. Psalm 37:7-8 (NIV) warns us not to "fret" when people malign us because it only leads to harm. We engage in "fretting" any time we obsess over the wrongs we have experienced at the hands of others. By replaying these incidents we deepen the wound, causing ourselves further pain and injury. What begins as pain ultimately becomes anger. The Hebrew word for *fret* actually means "to glow or blaze up."[39] When we end up becoming hot under the collar over the hurtful actions of others, we are inclined to turn our feelings of anger or injustice into actions directed against the other person. While holding someone else accountable for their actions in a hurtful situation is reasonable, attempting to "get back" at them is not.

Paul warned: "Dear friends, never take revenge. Leave that to the righteous anger of God. For the Scriptures say, 'I will take revenge; I will pay them back,' says the Lord" (Romans 12:19). We sabotage our serenity whenever we attempt, by way of revenge, to counterfeit God's rightful job of settling a score. When it comes to other people, God is able to discern what we cannot. Because He has the ability to look into the heart, He understands what motivates hurtful behavior and whether it is intentional or uncalculated. He is aware of the scars this sinful world has left on their heart, just as He is aware of those we carry on our own, and He will take all of this into account as He works to "make all things right." More often than I like to admit, while under the influence of my hurting emotions I have made assumptions about another's behavior, jumped to conclusions, and taken punitive actions to right my feelings that ended up hampering my serenity in the long run. The only action that is guaranteed to lead to living serenity is to "let go and let God" make all things right.

God is qualified to make things right in ways that we are not. He is capable of changing hearts and is able to employ the convicting power of His Spirit to accomplish a task which is far beyond our abilities. We are helped to maintain serenity when we remember that God works differently in different people. First Corinthians

12:6 (NIV) reminds us, "there are different kinds of working, but in all of them and in everyone it is the same God at work." God's methods for bringing about change may not be the ones I would employ, yet because He can judge righteously and I cannot, He is qualified to determine what approach is right for each individual. Because change occurs first within the heart and is then translated into action, it will not be obvious to me that God is making something right within someone else until later in the process. My job is to trust that even when change in another person is not apparent to me, God is still at work because that is what Scripture teaches. In the meantime, while I am waiting for things to be made right within someone else, God can be shielding and protecting me from further harm. With God's help it is possible for me to experience well-being and serenity even when people around me remain in their addiction or choose not to change.

While God is more concerned with building character by making all things right on the inside rather than changing circumstances on the outside, there are no circumstances that He cannot change. There is no person, place, or thing that is beyond His reach. There are no hopeless or impossible scenarios where God is concerned. Scripture records a vast array of circumstances in which God used diverse elements to accomplish His purposes and "make all things right." He used confusion, panic, insomnia, deep sleep, blindness, fire, ditches of water, lightening, and earthquakes to achieve certain outcomes. He used ravens, goats, lions, quail, fish, and oxen to fulfill His intentions, even causing a donkey to talk on one occasion. He caused fortress walls to crumble, chariot wheels to malfunction, the sun to stand still, rain to begin or cease, and winds to part the sea. He produced offspring in the infertile, changed the hearts of pagan kings, used dreams to warn of danger, turned curses into blessings, and made the invisible realm visible. He even managed to use capital punishment, as in the crucifixion, to accomplish good. He rescues, delivers, saves, shields, protects, redeems, restores, and renews in order to make "all things right."

In spite of God's ability to dramatically alter circumstances, there are times when He chooses not to change them. I am thinking of a young man's anguished prayer in a garden. Jesus implored His

Father to offer another solution to the world's problem of sin and change the dire circumstance He faced. The answer was "no," but His Father sent Him comfort in the form of an angel who brought Him strength (Luke 22:43). In reference to God's actions, Paul said: "He who did not spare his own Son, but gave him up for us all—how will he not also, along with him, graciously give us all things?" (Romans 8:32 NIV) My serenity is enriched whenever I realize that even when God does not change my circumstances, I can trust Him to provide all the comfort, strength, and grace I need to sustain me while I am in it.

Someone once said, "Never place a period where God has placed a comma."[40] As God's only Son, bloodied and beaten, stumbled down the path to Calvary, I doubt that it occurred to the crowds along the road that God was about to make all things right—once and for all. To those bystanders that day, Jesus was just another "dead man walking." And as they left the scene of the crucifixion smugly "high fiving" each other, the chief priests must have congratulated themselves for finally putting a period on the life of the man they considered a "wannabe" messiah. And during those long, agonizing hours between His crucifixion and resurrection, Christ's disciples must have speculated in disbelief as to why God had placed a period on a promising ministry that was just gaining momentum. It was just a comma; God's most magnificent work with regard to making *all* things right for *all* people was accomplished with a "no."

This is something for me to serenely ponder as I allow God to determine how and when to make all things right in my life.

Deborah Galasso

"That You Will Make All Things Right" and Me

I have always been a big fan of keeping a journal of my recovery, not just because it helps me to process life issues, but also because it serves as a record regarding how God is making all things right. Over the course of the last twenty-three years that I have been keeping a journal, God has made far many more things right than can be mentioned here. He has changed me in my circumstances by bringing comfort, revelation, and sustaining power; and He has at times changed my circumstances as well. It is both a joy and strength to have these memories of how God has "righted" my life.

As I read through my journals in an effort to find a meaningful example for this section, there was a particular incident that stood out. Prior to my daughter's graduation from college, she had a misunderstanding with her godmother. She phoned her to make amends, her apology was accepted, and we thought that the matter was resolved. However, the next day we received a message from her saying that she would not be attending my daughter's graduation at the end of that week. Our efforts to rectify the situation were of no avail. I knew that my daughter would be heartbroken when she learned of her godmother's decision, and I was feeling distressed by it also.

In truth, distressed did not begin to describe my response. I felt more like a mother grizzly bear protecting her cub! I was outraged, perplexed, inconsolable, and confused. I was crestfallen that the most praiseworthy achievement of my daughter's young life would be marred by sorrow; but most of all, I was just plain powerless. I couldn't protect my daughter's heart and I couldn't change her godmother's. I wanted to lash out at the person responsible for my pain, but I knew that this would simply damage things further. Besides, the Serenity Prayer encouraged me to allow God to make all things right. Was I willing to exchange my peace of mind for a moment of giving someone a piece of mine?

We decided to refrain from giving my daughter the bad news as she was in the middle of taking her final exams. I went on making plans for her graduation party, but the excitement had been replaced by melancholy, punctuated with intermittent crying jags. While I was struggling through the gamut of my emotions, I received a phone call from our pastor regarding an upcoming church board meeting. Realizing from the tone of my voice that something was troubling me, he inquired as to what was going on and listened patiently as I poured out my heart. After offering me encouragement, he ended by praying a beautiful prayer that took into consideration the needs of all parties involved. That prayer lifted my spirits, but knowing that God was aware of my need for comfort and provided that phone call at just the right time inspired me even more. It was as though God was saying, "Deborah, I've got My eyes on you. I hear your concerns and I know what you are going through. I'm collecting your tears in a bottle, and I am the God who can and will comfort you."

The following day my sister phoned me to share a devotion that she had read that morning. It emphasized how God is aware of the persecution we experience and holds people accountable for the harm they do to others. God was sending me another message: I didn't need to be concerned with justice because He was perfectly capable of handling that concern of mine. I was thankful for that bit of scriptural revelation and especially grateful for my sister's concern and care. Since we now had an extra ticket to the graduation ceremony, I was able to invite my sister to attend. As we stood side by side the morning of graduation and watched my daughter march in, my sister turned to me with tears in her eyes and said, "I'm sorry that her godmother isn't here, but I'm so glad that I got to come." And in that moment, I realized that God had made something right for my sister by providing her with that opportunity. Ultimately, the people who were meant to gratefully share my daughter's big day were all there.

It is remarkable how God is always at work making things right. Even before I am aware that things are going south, He is laying out a plan. From the moment this incident occurred, one of the things I had been asking God to do was to graciously protect my daughter's heart. Weeks earlier, she had lamented that she wouldn't be able to attend her cousin's graduation party the week after her own, because she had to attend a wedding. That seemed unfortunate at the time, but as things transpired it turned out to be a blessing. God spared her "sorrow upon sorrow" as she did not have to witness her godmother attending her cousin's party when she failed to attend hers.

After her party, I told my daughter what had taken place and she was understandably saddened. It gave us the chance to talk about the importance of forgiveness, and she learned a valuable life lesson that day and so did I. Although I may never have the same esteem for this person that I once possessed, I am happy to report that I am not eaten up with bitterness and hatred or full of thoughts of malice and revenge. On the contrary, as I type these words, what I am most aware of is gratitude. Although I wish that my daughter had been spared that arrow to the heart, I saw once again that God can take a painful situation and cause good to result.

Decades of journal entries testify to the truth of Second Corinthians 9:8 (NIV) which says, "And God is able to bless you abundantly, so that in all things at all times, having all that you need, you will abound in every good work." My serenity is alive and well because God makes all things right.

"That You Will Make All Things Right" and You

1. In what ways have you experienced God making all things right in your life?

____
____
____
____

2. What are some methods God has used to help you be "all right" during a difficult situation?

____
____
____
____
____
____

3. What are some methods God has used to change your circumstances?

____
____
____
____

4. How has God taken a bad circumstance in your life and caused good to result?

____
____
____
____

5. Are there currently situations in your life that you are attempting to make right when you need to "let go and let God" instead?

____
____
____
____

6. Have you ever been in a situation where "all things right" for someone else caused pain or difficulty for you?

____

____

____

____

7. Do you struggle with trying to "figure God out"? How does this show up?

____

____

____

____

8. Who is praying for you during times of difficulty?

____

____

____

____

9. Has God ever said "no" and yet still made all things right for you?

____

____

____

____

10. What do the following Scriptures reveal regarding the methods God uses to make you "all right" in difficult circumstances? (Psalm 145:14; Isaiah 30:21; Isaiah 41:10; Isaiah 65:24; Lamentations 3:58; Ezekiel 36:26-27; 1 Corinthians 10:13; 2 Corinthians 1:3-4, 20-22; 2 Corinthians 7:5-6; 2 Corinthians 9:8; 2 Timothy 3:16-17; 1 Peter 2:23)

____

____

____

____

____

____

____

____

11. What do the following Scriptures indicate regarding the variety of ways in which God acts on your behalf? (Genesis 39:5, 23; 2 Samuel 22:33; 2 Chronicles 20:15; Ezra 7:6; Psalm 66:5; Proverbs 16:7; Isaiah 26:12; Isaiah 42:16; Luke 18:7-8; 1 Corinthians 3:7; 2 Thessalonians 1:6; 2 Timothy 1:12; 2 Timothy 4:18; 2 Peter 2:9; Jude 24)

____

____

____

____

____

____

____

____

12. What do the following Scriptures teach regarding how God changes impossible circumstances? (Exodus 3:19-21; Ezra 6:22; Nehemiah 13:2; Jeremiah 32:17; Jeremiah 33:10-11; Luke 18:27; Acts 23:12-22; Romans 4:17; Ephesians 2:4-5)

____

____

____

____

____

____

____

____

13. What do the following Scriptures indicate regarding the ways in which God sustains us during difficulty? (Deuteronomy 1:29-31; Deuteronomy 2:7; 1 Chronicles 28:20; Psalm 48:14; Psalm 54:4; Psalm 119:50; Psalm 119:116; Hebrews 1:3)

____

____

____

____

____

____

____

____

14. What do the following Scriptures demonstrate regarding how God uses revelation to "make all things right"? (Amos 3:6-7; Luke 24:45; Galatians 2:2; Ephesians 1:17; Philippians 3:15; 2 Timothy 2:7)

____

____

____

____

____

____

15. What do the following Scriptures reveal regarding God's timing? (Ecclesiastes 3:1; Ecclesiastes 3:11; Luke 1:20; Luke 4:29-30; Luke 12:11-12; John 10:39; Galatians 6:9; Philippians 1:6; 1 Peter 5:6)

____

____

____

____

____

____

____

____

16. What idea from this chapter do you plan to put into practice?

____

____

____

____

Chapter Seventeen: If I Surrender to Your Will

The assurance that God will make all things right in our lives inspires serenity, however there is one condition. The Serenity Prayer indicates that God makes all things right *if* we will surrender to His will. How astonishing it is to realize that the only thing that can in essence limit our limitless God is the "if" of surrender. That little word "if" becomes a big question mark on the path to serenity. It is such a small word, yet it can become a considerable obstacle to living serenity.

Surrender is defined as giving up possession upon demand or compulsion.[41] I think that if God had a dictionary, it would contain a slightly different definition. God wants us to surrender to His will, but not on demand or under compulsion. That is because although our God is in control of all things, He is not controlling; He does not force His will on us. By endowing us with free will, God removed the option of surrender under compulsion in favor of surrender by choice. God loves the "if" contained in the Serenity Prayer because it represents our ability to choose His will over our own, and thereby demonstrate our love for Him.

I often wonder why I have such a struggle with surrender. Perhaps it is partly because surrender denotes giving up, and in that sense it seems like failure. Having lived in a culture that worships self-sufficiency, I have been brainwashed by the idea that one should never give up. When I think of surrender, I picture soldiers being marched off—hands held high in the air and heads hung in defeat. In twelve-step programs the idea of surrender is encapsulated in the slogan "let go and let God." As practical and truthful as this phrase is,

I must admit that the image of dangling from a considerable height and then suddenly letting go to do a free fall into space is pretty scary. It is no wonder I struggle with the concept of surrender, having attached so many negative notions to it. I overcome these negative perceptions when I realize that surrender is not failure, defeat, or weakness. On the contrary, surrendering into the loving hands of God is actually a positive thing; after all, I can't free fall if I am already resting in His hands.

The first step in learning to surrender is to relax my grip on the problem and take my hands off the solution. What this looks like in everyday life is that I stop being attached to certain outcomes, methods, or deadlines. Over and over again in my journey of recovery, I have found that it is the act of surrender that precedes changes in circumstances. I can fret, worry, scheme, and manipulate, and little changes except my level of frustration. It is only when I finally come to the end of my self-will and say, "Okay, Lord. Your will be done," that circumstances begin to change.

There is an abundance of positive change that God wants to bring to my life that requires surrender on my part. Just like the lame man Jesus encountered beside the pool at Bethesda, too often I am willing to settle for simply being able to walk again, when God wants to bring the kind of healing that would have me leaping, skipping, and running. I am content to simply have my addiction under control, when God wants to adjust and enrich my inner character. Because I don't mind covering the same familiar ground, I remain unwittingly stuck, working the first three steps again and again. While I am waltzing around, God is patiently waiting to teach me a new dance that requires some different, more complicated steps.

With regard to the status quo, God says, "But forget all that—it is nothing compared to what I am going to do. For I am about to do something new. See, I have already begun! Do you not see it? I will make a pathway through the wilderness. I will create rivers in the dry wasteland" (Isaiah 43:18-19). While I may be blithely stuck in the parched wasteland of my past, God wants to do something fresh and unique in my life. He wants to take me on an uncharted course through the desert into places I have never explored, on a road I have never traveled. Freedom, serenity, and new life can be found along the way, and all that is required is my cooperation by embracing the "if" of surrender.

God laments my struggle with the question of surrender just as much I do. The Living Bible version of Isaiah 1:18-19 has God describing in vivid terms the fresh start He wants to give people and ends with the words: "If you will only let me help you." Surrender and willingness go hand in hand. Jesus grieved what could have been but was not because of a lack of surrender. Matthew 23:37 records Jesus mourning over the city of Jerusalem, "How often I have wanted to gather your children together as a hen protects her chicks beneath her wings, but you wouldn't let me." When I read these words I wonder how many times unwillingness has prevented me from experiencing the comfort, protection, and nurture God wanted to provide. By maintaining my grip on self-will, I disengage from not only God's will, but also from the comfort that relationship with Him brings.

As we wrestle with the "if" of surrender, it helps to remember that surrender is a process that does not come naturally to people who have an inherent need to be in control. Romans 8:7 says, "For the sinful nature is always hostile to God. It never did obey God's laws, and it never will." As discussed in earlier chapters, self-will, not surrender, is our natural state of being. It is encouraging to read David's words in Psalm 143:10: "Teach me to do your will, for you are my God." Here is the man whom God described as being a man after His own heart, who just like the rest of us had to learn to do God's will (1 Samuel 13:14). While the Serenity Prayer's admonition to surrender to God's will may sound like a one-time decision, learning to surrender is actually a lifelong process. As with so many areas of our recovery, surrender is a moment-by-moment decision.

It is gratifying to realize that God doesn't mind that we have to learn to surrender. He is a patient teacher whose only prerequisite into His classroom is a willingness to learn. Willingness goes a long way with God. If we find that we are not surrendered to His will but are willing to move in that direction, God will help us to get to the place of surrender. In fact, God is even able to work with our unwillingness if we request His assistance. Philippians 2:13 says: "For God is working in you, giving you the desire and the power to do what pleases him." God's ability to work with unwillingness is repeated in Hebrews 13:21, which says that God can initiate in us what is pleasing to Him, thereby enabling us to do His will. There have been many times in my recovery when I have been unwilling to do God's will, but by admitting that to Him and expressing a desire to become willing, He has helped me to do so. Even unwillingness is not an obstacle for God.

What the Serenity Prayer refers to as "surrender" Scripture refers to as "wholeheartedness." The characteristic of wholehearted devotion is important to God. When David turned over the reins of the kingdom of Israel to Solomon, he encouraged his son to serve God with his "whole heart and a willing mind" (1 Chronicles 28:9). Because they followed Him wholeheartedly, Joshua and Caleb were the only two adults involved in the exodus from Egypt whom God allowed to enter the Promised Land (Numbers 32:11-12). Wholeheartedness matters to God because it reflects the truth of the Shema, the Jewish confession of faith instituted at the time of Moses, which says: "Listen, O Israel! The Lord is our God, the Lord alone. And you must love the Lord your God with all your heart, all your soul, and all your strength. And you must commit yourselves wholeheartedly to these commands that I am giving you today" (Deuteronomy 6:4-6). It was just this commandment that Jesus cited as the most important of all (Matthew 22:37-38). When we love God wholeheartedly, we demonstrate our love by choosing His will above our own. If God has our whole heart, then He has our will also.

While many people attend seminars, read self-help books, and hire life coaches to help uncover the purpose for their lives, Scripture is clear that we all share the same purpose—to do the will of God. Paul explained that God's will is good, pleasing, and perfect (Romans 12:2). Before recovery, we thought we knew what was best for us and we were certainly motivated by pleasing ourselves. The self-will that motivated our behavior only served to feed our addiction, eventually leaving us spiritually and morally bankrupt. When self-will is at odds with God's will, His will for us will always be best because it has our utmost spiritual and character growth in mind.

Too often we allow the importance of "knowing" God's will to become an obstacle to actually "doing" God's will. God's will is far less mysterious than we think. After all, there is a whole book called the Bible devoted to identifying exactly what comprises His will for people. Within its pages, wherever we see an action verb such as "be," "do," "walk," "submit," "stand," or "live," to name just a few, it is an indication of God's will for us. With this in mind, some of the things that we know are God's will include rejoicing in the Lord, obeying His commands, doing good works, loving others, telling the truth, sharing with others, giving to God's work, serving others, and paying our taxes! While God has both a general and specific will for people, we can end up wasting far too much time pondering God's specific plan for us while neglecting the importance of practicing the general. Micah succinctly summed up the general will of God when He wrote: "...the Lord has told you what is good, and this is what he requires of you: to do what is right, to love mercy, and to walk humbly with your God" (Micah 6:8).

The challenge that serenity seekers face with regard to surrendering to God's will is that it is an either/or proposition: we either act on His will or we act on our own. Jesus invites us to follow, not lead. Followers take direction. If we desire to experience the same serenity which characterized His life, then we must be willing to take up our cross as He did and embrace the concept of death to self-will. This is a painful prospect.

The good news regarding this rigorous type of surrender is that it ultimately leads to life. Jesus said, "Very truly I tell you, unless a kernel of wheat falls to the ground and dies, it remains only a single seed. But if it dies, it produces many seeds" (John 12:24 NIV). Contained within the seemingly dead outer hull of a seed, all the genetic material needed to produce an abundance of seeds lies dormant, awaiting just the right conditions for growth. It is not until the seed falls to the ground that the outer hull dies away, and with the help of water and light, new life can occur. Surrender is a lot like the beginning of the life cycle of a seed. As we die to self-will, the potential for new life that follows surrender to God's will becomes a reality. Embracing His will releases the spiritual DNA that reproduces Christ's character within us, removing our defects of character while at the same time changing our hearts and spirits.

In our journey toward living serenity, every one of us will face the "if" of surrender time and time again. Scripture provides a record of the pivotal "ifs" faced by God's people throughout history. King David's "if" came when the son produced from his illicit affair with Bathsheba died. During the child's illness, he implored God to change His will and allow the child to live. He stopped eating and sleeping for a full week. His behavior so distressed his servants that when the child finally died, they were afraid to tell him. But once he learned what God's will was, he simply surrendered to it by getting up off the ground, tending to his hygiene, going to the temple to worship, and returning home for a meal (2 Samuel 12:14-23). Had David not surrendered to God's will, if he had instead become embittered, he would have been unable to pen the words: "Restore me to the joy of Your salvation and sustain me with a willing spirit" (Psalm 51:12 NASB). In fact, without his willingness to surrender, half the book of Psalms would not have been written, as much of what David wrote in them spoke to the importance of trust and surrender.

King Saul failed to surrender to God's will and ended up losing his kingdom to God's chosen replacement, David. Although he had been clearly instructed by the prophet Samuel to wait, Saul, motivated by desperation, took matters into his own hands by offering sacrifices he was not qualified to offer. Because Old Testament prophets served as the mouthpieces for God, Saul's failure to follow Samuel's instruction was actually a form of opposition to God's will (1 Samuel 13:8-14). On the other hand, Queen Esther, who faced the desperate possibility of annihilation of the entire Jewish population, chose to surrender to God's will by undertaking the potentially fatal business of approaching her husband the king without a formal invitation. Her poignant words of surrender are recorded in Esther 4:16: "... though it is against the law, I will go in to see the king. If I must die, I must die." She did not die, the Jews were saved, and the festival of Purim is a lasting reminder of what her act of surrender achieved.

Jonah's decision to pursue his own direction rather than surrender to God's will landed him on a boat headed into a violent storm. After being thrown overboard, his big "if" came in the belly of a whale, where he acknowledged to God that he would make good on all the vows he had made (Jonah 2:9). Because Jonah ultimately surrendered to God's will that he "carry the message," as we refer to it in recovery circles, one hundred and twenty thousand people came to believe in God. Shadrach, Meshach, and Abednego were so surrendered to God's will that they defied King Nebuchadnezzar's decree to worship his image. The king's punishment was to threaten to cremate them alive, to which they responded: "If we are thrown into the blazing furnace, the God whom we serve is able to save us. He will rescue us from your power, Your Majesty. But even if he doesn't, we want to make it clear to you, Your Majesty, that we will never serve your gods or worship the gold statue you have set up" (Daniel 3:17-18). The king threw them into the furnace anyway, but God preserved their life. Through a courageous act of surrender on the part of those three men, that narcissistic king ended up learning an important lesson about the one true God.

The stories of Sarah of the Old Testament and Mary of the New Testament are remarkably similar, yet had vastly different outcomes. Both received the news that they would bear a promised child, however Sarah received her news with a scornful laugh while Mary received hers with a humble heart. Frustrated by years of childlessness, Sarah had impatiently forced a solution which, although it was culturally sanctioned, was not God's solution for the problem of her infertility. The decision to have a surrogate child through the union of her husband and Hagar, their servant, ultimately left her resentful and embittered and Hagar brokenhearted and homeless (Genesis 16:1-8; 18:10-15; 21:8-16). On the other hand, Mary faced her big "if" with an attitude of surrender. Unwed at the time and facing certain disapproval from her family, friends, and fiancé, it would have been understandable if she had questioned God's will. Instead, she humbly accepted God's will by declaring, "I am the Lord's servant. May everything you have said about me come true" (Luke 1:38).

Christ's big "if" occurred in the garden of Gethsemane. The Gospels record the moving scene of God's only Son struggling with surrender. We know that it was a struggle because the Gospel accounts describe Him as being sorrowful, troubled, overwhelmed, deeply distressed, anguished, and sweating profusely (Matthew 26:37-38; Mark 14:33; Luke 22:44). Luke records the words of His earnest prayer: "Father, if you are willing, please take this cup of suffering away from me. Yet I want your will to be done, not mine" (Luke 22:42). Jesus, who was once approached by a diseased man saying, "If You are willing, You can make me clean," to which He replied "I am willing" (Luke 5:12-13 NASB), was now beseeching the Father He loved for willingness to find another way. In spite of His intense emotions, He chose the "if" of surrender because there was nothing more important to Him than fulfilling His Father's will.

Although I have read the account of Christ's struggle in the garden countless times and I know the outcome, I still weep my way through it, wishing along with Him that there could have been a different solution, that the outcome for saving humankind did not require His death on a cross. I weep even more when I consider what would have become of this sinful world had He not surrendered. Christ's willingness to surrender reminds me that the outcome of such bold choices will always produce results that are both far reaching and beyond my immediate comprehension.

What is evident from these examples is that surrender to God's will accomplishes great things for His kingdom, while failure to do so carries consequences of its own. God uses surrendered people to carry His message and accomplish His plans in a sinful world. Mordecai, Esther's uncle, understood this truth when he warned her that if she should choose against God's will, God would find another way to deliver the Jews, but she would miss out on the blessing of using her God-given station as queen to fulfill His purpose (Esther 4:14). Scripture is full of "if/then" passages which indicate the blessings that follow surrender to God's will, as well as the consequences of following our own. As difficult as death to self-will can be, blessing ultimately follows surrender as evidenced by Paul's statement, "If we die with him, [then]we will also live with him" (2 Timothy 2:11, additions mine).

God's overall will for people is that we live in a state of ongoing, continual surrender. This means that we surrender the little problems and not just the big ones, and our mistakes as well as our dilemmas. Living in a surrendered state means that we obey His will even when we cannot make sense of it. Jesus once directed Peter to go fishing in a certain part of the lake. After a long, hard night of fishing without any success, Peter was probably both exhausted as well as discouraged. He must have wondered why Jesus would ask him to take such a seemingly futile action, yet Scripture indicates that Peter responded by letting down the nets simply because Jesus said to. Peter surrendered to Christ's will, and the outcome ended up being an astonishing catch of fish unlike any Peter had ever witnessed before (Luke 5:1-10). The kind of surrender that accomplishes astonishing results in our lives comes from a place of obedience based on "because Jesus said to," and our only hope of living in such a simple state is through repeated application of the principles of the Serenity Prayer.

The decision to live a surrendered life will often mean learning to wait—a pretty tall order for impulsive people like us! Sometimes we wait because we are in need of God's direction regarding His will, and at other times we wait because God's timetable differs from our own. The difference between God's timetable and our own is remarkable when we consider Ezekiel 36:8 in which God says of the exiled nation of Israel "they will be coming home again soon." To me, *soon* means sometime this week; to God it meant over half a century. That is why David, who as we have seen became seasoned at waiting on God's will, encouraged us to wait patiently, expectantly, and wholeheartedly (Psalms 5:3; 40:1). Serenity increases in proportion to our ability to learn to sit quietly and prayerfully in God's waiting room.

One thing is certain: the commitment to surrender will always produce seeds of serenity that will reap a harvest. When I have loosened my grip on self-will, relinquished the struggle for control, and placed His will at the center of my life, my soul is at rest and it is in that soul-rest that I find living serenity.

"If I Surrender to Your Will" and Me

Until I ran across this line in the Serenity Prayer, I couldn't understand my reluctance to sing certain types of songs during the worship service at church. I was fine with the songs about God's greatness. I loved the songs about God's saving power, but the songs about surrender? I just couldn't bring myself to sing words implying that I would do whatever God asked me to do, because I knew that it would lack sincerity. I feared that if I wholeheartedly sang words of surrender, there would be some kind of drastic test to validate my candor. I equated surrender with willingness to lose everything I held dear. I was convinced that God would test me, just as He had tested Abraham's willingness to put Isaac on the altar, and in spite of the fact that their story had a happy ending, I didn't want to go there. So I held surrender to God's will at arm's distance for a long time, which hindered the development of my serenity.

Just as with every other area of my recovery, my journey to willing surrender was a process. There were many big "ifs" along the way—some that I recognized at the time and others that I recognized only through the benefit of hindsight. The first "if" came when I revealed my relapsed state to my pastor and encouraged him to start a church-based recovery group for people like me. It was risky business to reveal this as I had hidden the truth about my addiction from everyone, especially my church family. Through involvement with community-based twelve-step groups, I had enjoyed varying periods of sobriety in my life. But because I hadn't truly come to terms with the idea of powerlessness, I kept returning to my addiction. I was shocked when my pastor listened to my desperate request and suggested that my past experience with the twelve steps qualified me to start the group. I reasoned that he must have missed the part about my being in a relapsed state, so I reiterated that, to which he asked, "Do you want to recover?"

I said, "Yes, of course."

And he very wisely said, "Then start the group."

The "if" of starting a group required commitment, and I was one of the most uncommitted people I knew. In fact, the only thing I had been one hundred percent committed to was the practice of my addiction. Based on my experiences with sobriety in the past, I doubted that I would be successful over the long run. True to my uncommitted nature, I set the group up so that it could be led by anyone, just in case I needed to bail out at some point. See how uncommitted I was? Yet in spite of this, group members still looked to me to be the leader, and being in that position actually proved helpful in maintaining my commitment when the going got tough. There were many times when I wanted to give up and turn back, but I didn't because I believed that the group members, as well as my pastor, were counting on me. While this is definitely not the recommended way to start a twelve-step group, it worked in my case because God saw that while I couldn't make a commitment to myself, my untreated codependency insured that I would not want to let others down. God knew exactly what it would take for me to recover and the level of accountability that I required.

Several months into the life of the group, a flyer arrived at the church advertising a Christian recovery conference and my pastor thought I should attend. This conference outlined a whole program for establishing a Christ-centered, church-based recovery program. It was exciting stuff, but daunting nonetheless, as it required a much higher level of commitment in terms of time and energy. I was standing at a crossroad and I sensed that God was saying to me, "What do you want to do? Do you want to wholeheartedly surrender to My will and be a part of this, or should I find someone else?" It was my second big "if."

I decided that I did want to surrender, but at that point in my journey it was still more about surrendering with my head, rather than my heart. I believed that participating in the development of the recovery program was God's will for me, but I was surrendering because it was the right thing to do rather than as an act of love. Recalling this period of time reminds me of the Scripture which says that toward the end of His time on earth Jesus set out "resolutely" for Jerusalem (Luke 9:51). I was surrendering resolutely, but not wholeheartedly. Yet because surrender is a process, at times we surrender by sheer determination until we are enabled through God's grace to reach the point of wholeheartedness. As I returned to that recovery conference each year, God patiently worked on the attitude of my heart until I was able to come to a place of wholehearted surrender to Him.

While I initially thought that surrendering to God's will was mostly a matter of time and commitment, it actually was much, much more. Surrendering to God's will required that I forfeit my pride and inclination toward self-gain. While my motives for service may have seemed altruistic to others, they were actually quite selfish and self-centered in the beginning. I liked controlling and managing things, so I had to learn to share responsibility. I was a natural-born teacher who enjoyed being center stage, so I had to learn to give others the opportunity to grow in their teaching abilities also. If I wanted to be surrendered to God's will, then I had to learn to curb my impulsiveness, rely on His timing, and trust in His ability to provide every resource needed to grow His ministry, His way.

I had to remind myself continually that it was His ministry, not mine. Surrender meant wholehearted commitment to Him, not the recovery ministry; to attempt it any other way would have proved unsuccessful. That's because God's plans are always so much greater than I realize. Initially, I had simply wanted to recover within a Christian setting, and I hoped that maybe a handful of other people in my church would want to come along on the journey with me. God, on the other hand, had a vision for scores of changed lives in people, who, once changed, would carry the message of His grace and freedom to others still struggling. All that was required on my part was to surrender to His will to the best of my ability—one "if" at a time.

That tentative commitment began more than twelve years ago, and while today there is no doubt of my commitment, God is still bringing me to deeper levels of surrender. There is a saying in twelve-step groups: "More will be revealed." As I meditated on this principle in the Serenity Prayer in preparation for writing this chapter, I became aware of how much further there is to go in terms of wholehearted surrender. I began to see that too often my usual method of surrendering is to say to God, "Okay, Lord, whatever You want." While on the surface this statement may sound as though I am giving God the right of way in my life, it actually implies that I am just tolerating His will. While this is a much more yielded state than where I first began, I cannot help but realize that in terms of my love for Him and His amazing grace to me, that statement seems a bit insulting. It is a response that is quite different from saying, "Yes, Lord, I want what You want," thereby embracing His will and wholeheartedly joining Him in His desires for me.

While I once feared what sincere surrender to God would require of me, I can honestly say that I have never had to let go of something I truly needed or relinquish something which He did not replace with something much more suitable. I am no longer as willing as I once was to wander around the wasteland of self-will, dying for a sip of living water, when my willingness to surrender allows Him to take me by the hand and lead me out. Remembering this motivates me toward getting to the place of surrender a little sooner, and ultimately that's where we both want me to be. Because when I want what He wants, there is nothing to fear and serenity prevails with surrender.

"If I Surrender to Your Will" and You

1. Do you wrestle with surrender?

2. What experiences in your recovery have required "dying to self"?

3. How has God worked with your unwillingness? How has willingness affected your recovery?

4. What consequences have you experienced related to following self-will versus God's will?

5. What big "ifs" of surrender have you faced in your recovery and what were the outcomes?

6. What do the following Scriptures tell you about the nature of God's will? (Isaiah 46:10-11; Isaiah 55:11; Matthew 6:10; Matthew 10:29; Acts 5:38-39; Galatians 1:3-4; Ephesians 1:5)

7. What do the following Scriptures reveal about dying to self-will? (Jeremiah 10:23; Mark 8:34; Luke 5:9-11; John 21:20-22; James 4:7; Revelation 2:26)

8. What do the following Scriptures indicate about the importance of willingness? (Psalm 143:10; Jeremiah 6:17-19; Matthew 23:2-4; Hebrews 12:9)

9. What do the following Scriptures indicate about the importance of wholeheartedness? (Joshua 14:8-11; 1 Kings 8:23; 1 Chronicles 29:9; 2 Chronicles 15:15; 2 Chronicles 19:8-9; 2 Chronicles 25:2; 2 Chronicles 31:21; Romans 6:17-18; Ephesians 6:7-8)

10. What do the following Scriptures say about the importance of waiting? (Psalm 33:20; Psalm 40:1; Proverbs 20:22; Isaiah 64:4; Lamentations 3:25-26; Micah 7:7)

11. What big "ifs" did the following people face, and did they evidence surrender or self-will? (Genesis 12:1-5; Hosea 1:2-3; 3:1-3; Matthew 1:18-25; Luke 1:8-20; Luke 5:27-28; John 6:66-69; 2 Corinthians 12:7-10)

12. What do the following Scriptures reveal regarding God's will for you? (Romans 13:1-3, 7-10; Ephesians 4:22-5:6; Ephesians 5:8-11, 15-17; 1 Thessalonians 4:3-8; 1 Thessalonians 5:12-22; Titus 2:3-8; Hebrews 10:36; 1 Peter 2:15)

13. What do the following "if/then" Scriptures tell you about the consequences of surrendering to God's will? (Isaiah 48:18; John 14:15; John 15:7; 1 Corinthians 11:31; 2 Corinthians 5:17; Galatians 6:9; 1 John 2:1; 1 John 5:14; Revelation 3:20)

14. What idea from this chapter do you plan to put into practice?

Chapter Eighteen: So That I May Be Reasonably Happy in This Life

As I practice the truths contained in the lines of the Serenity Prayer, I find that each and every one has increased my ability to experience living serenity. Yet on a practical level, none have changed the way I approach life as much as the idea of "reasonably happy." Prior to discovering the prayer, I didn't realize that I was applying standards to my life that were unreasonable. I was clueless to the fact that "reasonable" didn't exist in my frame of reference. Reasonable was not a high enough standard for me; I was too busy trying to make my life perfect. As I saw it, reasonable meant ordinary and I wanted to be extraordinary. Reasonable meant mediocre and I was too busy trying to be amazing. I had to be—my barely-there self-esteem depended on it.

At some point in my life, I had begun to believe that perfection was the only solution for a severely impaired self-concept. If I could just be "perfect enough," those nagging feelings of self-doubt and inferiority would disappear for good. The idea of striving for perfection had been deeply ingrained in me by the legalistic standards of the church in which I grew up. I viewed perfectionism as a positive thing, a force for good in my life. I never imagined that it was actually a curse; and that as long as I was driven by the need to be perfect, I could never experience an abiding sense of serenity.

At first glance, perfectionism may appear to be a positive thing. After all, wouldn't the world be a much better place if everyone were striving to do their best? Unfortunately, the drawback for people who are perfectionists is that they are oriented toward the negative instead of the positive. The glass is always half empty. There is always at least one thing that is not quite right. There is always something one could have done a little better. Given this orientation, one can never be satisfied that they have done their best. There was a time in my career when I taught continuing education workshops for nurses. Part of the board of registered nursing's requirements for granting credit for class attendance was that attendees complete an evaluation of the course and instructor. I could receive sixty evaluations that gave me high marks for my presentation skills, but I would focus instead on the one that found me lacking. It was impossible for me to ever feel "reasonably happy" given that unreasonable tendency.

The problem with perfectionists is not that they have high standards—it is that they have impossible standards. And while a perfectionist would agree intellectually that "people can't be perfect," their emotional response to imperfection would beg to differ. It would be one thing if perfectionists set the bar high for themselves only. Unfortunately, they expect others to live up to their impossibly high standards also. Because unrealistic expectations are simply premeditated resentments, perfectionists are destined to experience chronic disappointment and ongoing resentment, which will eventually be detrimental to their interpersonal relationships. Additionally, the inability to accept their own imperfections and shortcomings leaves the perfectionist vulnerable to blaming others, which only adds to interpersonal difficulties.

Because perfectionism has every bit of the "ism" of self-obsession contained in other addictions, it can hamper recovery. This is one of the reasons that the slogan "progress not perfection" is stressed in recovery groups. While progress is a reasonable place for us to focus our attention and expectations for ourselves, perfection is not. The need to be perfect obstructs the ability to admit to imperfection. This inability to admit to shortcomings and character defects blocks openness and, therefore, recovery. Every step we take toward change and maturity begins with the ability to admit. The belief that others either cannot or will not perform to the same high standards that they embrace keeps the perfectionist terminally stuck in the trap of "if I want the job done right, I must do it myself." The inability to ask for help, and the tendency to reject help that is offered, leads to isolation rather than the sense of community encouraged within recovery groups.

It is perfectly understandable that we humans desire perfection. Having originally been created in the image of our perfect God, we have a natural inclination toward wanting to reflect this perfection. When God created people, He placed them in a perfect world in which all of their needs were perfectly met. However, with free will came the possibility of imperfection, and that is just what happened when sin entered the picture. I have often heard people justify striving for perfection by quoting Matthew 5:48 in which Jesus says: "But you are to be perfect, even as your Father in heaven is perfect." In the Amplified Bible's version of this Scripture, "perfect" means "growing into complete maturity of godliness in mind and character." Scripture clearly teaches that no one is perfect except God, and that we cannot obtain perfection based on our own efforts. Instead, we are being made perfect by the work of the Holy Spirit in us. In that sense, it is not our efforts that produce perfection, but rather the result of God's work in us. This is the message of grace—that God does for us what we cannot do for ourselves. When we strive for perfection through our own efforts, we miss this priceless gift.

For recovering perfectionists like me, the Serenity Prayer's suggestion that we focus on attaining a state of being "reasonably happy" introduces a standard of living which offers the hope of finding serenity. If you look up the word *reasonable* in a thesaurus, you will see words like practical, sensible, wise, sound, credible, maintainable, suitable, and sane.[42] As we practice the standard of "reasonable," our lives become more balanced. We are no longer stuck, swinging back and forth between extremes of behavior. Rather than functioning in an ongoing state of exhaustion due to overcommitment of time, "reasonable" can become the new standard by which we plan our schedules. Instead of attempting to please others by complying with any and all requests, we can instead ask ourselves if the request is "reasonable" and decide to commit to only those that meet the "reasonable" standard. When we are confused we can ask, "Lord, is this a 'reasonable' course of action?"

When we focus on being "reasonably happy," we become happier because we stop focusing on being "relatively happy." Being "reasonably happy" means that we don't have to keep up with the Joneses; in fact, we don't have to keep up with other people at all. When we get stuck in the trap of determining our happiness on the basis of how we compare to others, we can never feel lasting happiness, let alone serenity. Comparing ourselves to other people is a guaranteed way to be reasonably unhappy because we are assured of coming up short at least fifty percent of the time. We will not have to look too far to find someone who has a bigger house, a better car, a higher paying job, a more advanced degree, or better behaved children. The other half of the time in this "more than, less than" orientation to happiness is not much better. Feeling happier about myself because someone else is worse off than I am not only lacks compassion, it isn't a useful or effective solution for the core issue of low self-esteem either.

The story that Jesus told of a land owner who hired day laborers illustrates the discontentment that results from making our serenity dependent on outside circumstances rather than internal factors. The contractor offered to pay the laborers a dollar for a day's work. He continued to hire more laborers right up until an hour before the workday ended. When the wages were paid, those hired earlier in the day became indignant that those who worked shorter hours by being hired later in the day received the same wage as they did. Initially when they were hired, the idea of working for one dollar seemed reasonable and they gladly accepted it. But in the end, when they compared their situation to the other workers, they became discontented (Matthew 20:1-15).

While we all experience the inclination to compare ourselves to others, Scripture instructs us to beware of this tendency. Jesus illustrated this idea during a poignant conversation with Peter in which He revealed a disturbing prophecy regarding what the future would hold for him. After hearing this revelation Peter, asked about what was in store for another disciple, to which Jesus replied, "What difference does it make? You need to focus on following Me" (John 21:18-22, my paraphrase). When we begin to compare our own journey of recovery and spiritual growth to someone else's, it distracts us from the particular plan God has for our life. We stop following and instead look longingly at what we think someone else has. If we wish to be reasonably happy, we cannot afford to rob ourselves of contentment by comparing our situation to another's. The only fair comparison that can be beneficial and contribute to being reasonably happy is "me today versus me yesterday"—am I moving toward God's spiritual goals for me or away from them?

If we desire to experience living serenity and be "reasonably happy in this life," then it is helpful to understand the biblical principle of contentment. Paul stressed the importance of *learning* to be content. In Philippians 4:11-13 (NIV) he wrote: "I am not saying this because I am in need, for I have learned to be content whatever the circumstances. I know what it is to be in need, and I know what it is to have plenty. I have learned the secret of being content in any and every situation, whether well fed or hungry, whether living in plenty or in want. I can do all this through him who gives me strength." I am relieved that Paul indicated that he was not born content but that even he, a wholly committed pillar of the church, had to learn contentment. As much as I wish that being content were my natural tendency, it is heartening to know that it is something that I can learn if I so desire. Because contentment is a form of serenity, the more I learn to be content, the more serenity I will experience.

To learn to be content, and subsequently "reasonably happy," we must be able to separate "needs" from "wants." As humans we have only a few basic, vital needs: food, shelter, and clothing. And while most of us would probably consider love and relationship to be vital, we actually can survive even in the absence of them. Everything beyond these needs that is necessary for survival can be considered wants or desires. Most of the time when I am feeling discontent, it is not because my basic needs are not met, it is because there is a "want" in my life that is unsatisfied. Whenever my serenity is disrupted because I am feeling frustrated or deprived by an unmet "want," it becomes restored when I remind myself that, at this moment in time, my basic needs are met.

When I am inclined to throw myself a pity party to celebrate the things that are lacking in my life, my sponsor begins to ask me a series of questions: "Did you eat today?" Did you have a bed to sleep in?" "When you woke up this morning, did you have a roof over your head?" "Did you drive to our appointment in your car?" Part of me hates it when she uses this approach on me, but it never fails to remind me that to be content, serene, and reasonably happy, I need to focus on what I have rather than what I believe I am lacking.

First Timothy 6:6-8 reminds us: "Yet true godliness with contentment is itself great wealth. After all, we brought nothing with us when we came into the world, and we can't take anything with us when we leave it. So if we have enough food and clothing, let us be content." This can be a difficult perspective to maintain while living in a society which is so consumption oriented. Needy people are consuming people. The purpose of the billions of dollars spent on advertising in this country is to convince us that our wants are actually needs. We must be careful to refrain from confusing the two if reasonable happiness is the desired outcome.

As a result of practicing the Serenity Prayer, I am learning to embrace the concept of reasonable. Acceptable, average, and balanced are the new perfect in my book. After all, even our God, who is a completely perfect Being, endorses the importance of "reasonable." Isaiah 1:18 (NASB) quotes Him as saying, "Come now, and let us reason together." "Reasonable" has become my new evaluation tool. I ask myself "reasonable" questions all the time. Do I have a reasonably good marriage or one that approximates a fairy tale? Is my house reasonably clean or can you eat off of the floor? Is this a reasonable amount of money to spend right now? Is this a reasonable amount of time to invest? Is this a reasonable thing for me to expect? What is a reasonable response in this situation? Is it reasonable to feel this way?

Interestingly enough, in spite of my fear that my life would become mediocre and lacking if I changed my standard from "being the best" to "being reasonable," quite the opposite has occurred. Not only do I enjoy my life much more, I also like myself much better. I am realizing that I do not have to be such a harsh taskmaster with myself, and when I do complete a project, I am able to take delight in it rather than pick it apart. I am more accepting of others and I do not need to pick them apart either, which has helped to improve my relationships tremendously. I am free to be reasonably happy and serene.

And in "this life," that is enough, given that I am physically separated from the God I love. I am a spiritual being, created to be in the presence of God. My citizenship is in heaven and I am eagerly awaiting my Savior (Philippians 3:20). This world is simply a temporary home, and until this situation is rectified, I can never experience perfection or be completely satisfied. Second Corinthians 5:2 (NIV) reminds me of this truth when it says, "Meanwhile we groan, longing to be clothed instead with our heavenly dwelling."

Because I'm living in the transitory land of "meanwhile," I'll just settle for being reasonably happy and the amazing amount of serenity it offers.

"So That I May Be Reasonably Happy in This Life" and Me

As I look back over my recovery, I can see that perfectionism was an addiction every bit as destructive to me as chemical dependency. As contradictory as it might seem, perfection fueled my chemical addiction. One of the reasons I used chemicals was to suppress the internal critic that kept me striving toward impossible expectations. The more I began to depend upon chemicals, the worse I felt about myself; the worse I felt about myself, the harder I tried to be perfect. I was stuck in a hopeless downward spiral.

Thank heaven that the Serenity Prayer introduced me to the concept of reasonable happiness. My expectations for both myself as well as life in general had been so unreasonable up to that point that it took a while to sort out what "reasonable" entailed. I had been using chemicals, not just to medicate my harsh internal critic, but also as a substitute for the happiness I was lacking. When I was high, I felt happier. Unfortunately, because addiction is progressive in nature, eventually I found that I was no longer content to "get" high; I wanted to "be" high. I thought that I should be supremely happy in this life and that chemicals were the best bet to deliver on this unrealistic expectation.

Once I began working a program of recovery and the problem of chemical dependency was arrested, I still had to confront the problem of perfectionism. I was surprised to find that it was much more difficult to give up than chemicals. The misery that chemicals had brought to my life was obvious, but with regard to perfection, the misery was much more subtle. I had a hard time saying to myself, "I'm doing the best I can," because I felt that I was capable of so much more. No matter how many steps forward I took, there was so much more work that needed to be done, so many areas of my life that still needed to be changed. It was impossible to feel content.

A turning point came during a recovery conference, when the keynote speaker encouraged us to be patient with ourselves. He recommended that we say to our internal critic, "Be nice to me, judge, because by the grace of God, I am doing my best." I realized during that talk that the only solution for my perfectionism was to apply God's grace to it. In fact, the only hope for recovery in any area in which I struggle is "by the grace of God."

The need to be perfect did not simply prevent me from being reasonable; it prevented me from accessing God's grace also. My best efforts will never achieve for me what His grace can and will accomplish on my behalf. There is no controlling God's grace; it changes me according to His timeline and purpose. My role is to simply admit, expect, trust, and wait patiently for it to be manifested in my life. The more willing I am to admit my shortcomings and need for His grace, the more opportunity there is for me to experience it. The moments in my recovery when I have felt the closest to Him, been the most aware of His presence, felt the most loved, and experienced the most grace, were when I admitted my utter hopelessness, helplessness, sickness, and need. Those moments are always painful and met with many tears, but the experience of grace which follows is pure joy.

It is not easy to be a recovering perfectionist. Perfectionism has skewed my orientation to the point that at times it is still difficult to answer the question, "What is reasonable?" I find myself longing for the day when I am fully recovered, but that day does not come. I become surprised and dismayed at the depth of my character defects. I overcome one to a certain extent, only to have it rear its ugly head at another time, with another person, in another situation. This causes my tendency toward "unreasonable" to kick in and I am inclined to begin thinking, "I am never going to get this."

It is at just those moments that I forget that the goal is to be "reasonably happy." Disillusioned, I sit down on the side of the Road to Recovery, and it seems reasonable to give up. But then along comes Jesus. He restores me to sanity by reminding me that He came for the sick, not the healthy, and that His grace is sufficient for whatever situation has brought me down. He reminds me that He does not expect me to be perfect—just committed to Him. It is a reasonable expectation and it never fails to get me on my feet again.

And because of His unreasonable, extravagant grace and the abundant serenity it brings, I am never without a reason to be "reasonably happy in this life."

"So That I May Be Reasonably Happy in This Life" and You

1. How does perfectionism hamper your serenity?

____

____

____

2. What relationship have you observed between perfectionism and resentment?

____

____

____

3. Do you have a tendency to compare yourself to others, and how does this affect you emotionally?

____

____

____

____

____

4. Do you consider yourself to be content? Why or why not?

____

____

____

____

____

5. What kind of "reasonable" standards could you apply to bring contentment and serenity to your life?

____

____

____

____

____

6. What explanation does Second Peter 2:7-8 give as to why you can only be reasonably happy in this life?

7. What do these Scriptures teach regarding the source of perfection? (2 Samuel 22:33; Psalm 119:96; Isaiah 26:3; 2 Corinthians 4:7; 2 Corinthians 12:9; Galatians 2:21; Galatians 5:5; Colossians 1:28; Hebrews 7:19, 28; Hebrews 10:14; Hebrews 12:2; James 3:2)

8. What do the following Scriptures tell you about contentment? (Psalm 103:2-5; Proverbs 13:25; Proverbs 19:23; Ecclesiastes 2:24-25; Ecclesiastes 3:13; Ecclesiastes 3:22; Ecclesiastes 4:8; Luke 3:14; Hebrews 13:5)

9. What does Scripture teach about the characteristics of reasonable people? Which of these do you exhibit? (Proverbs 12:16; Proverbs 13:16; Proverbs 14:8, 15, 18; Proverbs 15:5; Proverbs 22:3; Acts 17:2, 17; 1 Corinthians 13:11-12)

10. What does Scripture tell you about where it is reasonable to put your efforts? (Romans 14:19; 2 Corinthians 4:18; Galatians 3:3-5; Ephesians 4:3-6; Hebrews 12:14; 2 Peter 1:5-8; 2 Peter 3:14)

11. What idea from this chapter do you plan to put into practice?

Chapter Nineteen: And Supremely Happy with You Forever in the Next

What a wonderful way for the Serenity Prayer to close. After including such challenging concepts as powerlessness, hardship, and surrender, the prayer points toward a future filled with hope. Regardless of how difficult things may appear at times or what kind of unpleasant circumstances we may face, the future is not an unknown. In fact, it could not be brighter. Our happiness is guaranteed. And it is not just happiness that we can look forward to—it is supreme happiness lived out in the presence of the supreme God for eternity. Anticipating this truth cannot help but bring a sense of serenity to one's life.

The message of this line of the prayer is that we have a hopeful future. This reflects the truth found in Jeremiah 31:17, which says that God's plans for people are to give them a future hope. Proverbs 23:18 points to the eternal nature of this plan when it says, "You will be rewarded for this; your hope will not be disappointed." An attitude of hopefulness is vital to our emotional health and influences our ability to experience serenity. Hebrews 6:19 (NASB) tells us that hope is like an anchor for the soul. On the other hand, Proverbs 13:12 says that "hope deferred makes the heart sick." The presence or absence of hope has the power to influence the very core of one's being.

Given the profound ability to influence our sense of serenity and well-being, it is no wonder that the Bible encourages us to hold tightly to the hope we say we have (Hebrews 10:23). When God made the promise cited in Jeremiah 31:17 to the Israelites, they were still in captivity and exile in Babylon. He understood how important it was for them to have a future hope to help them endure the difficulties they were facing. Although their circumstances were dire, He was assuring them that the future was going to be better. What was true for the ancient Israelites is still true for us today. In spite of how things look to us at the moment, when we have an attitude of hope for the future, we find strength and encouragement for today.

Paul encouraged believers, "Think about the things of heaven, not the things of earth" (Colossians 3:2). In my attempts to recover, I have spent so much time focusing on overcoming the handicaps of the past that it is a pleasant alternative to focus instead on the reality of what is ahead. The anticipation of the supreme happiness that awaits me has the power to bring optimism to my attitude today. It reminds me of when I would tell my young son that we were going to a famous southern California amusement park. In his five-year-old mind, a trip to that happy kingdom was the zenith of supreme happiness. Each day as he looked forward to it, his whole attitude would reflect joyful anticipation.

For someone like me who has wasted far too much time anxiously anticipating the worst, the prospect of joyfully anticipating the future is a welcome change of outlook. I can be joyful and serene about the future because "everlasting joy" is exactly what I am promised (Isaiah 35:10). While in this life many of us may have worried about our finances, living paycheck to paycheck, wishing we had a rich uncle we could inherit from, in the next life we truly are heirs. James 2:5 tells us that we will "inherit the kingdom he promised to those who love him." Paul referred to it as a "glorious inheritance" (Ephesians 1:18), and Peter described it as a "priceless inheritance" that can never deteriorate or change (1 Peter 1:4). While wills can be changed and people can be disinherited, the inheritance that God has promised to us will be ours for eternity.

Supreme happiness lies ahead for us because physical separation from God will no longer exist and we will spend our eternal future in His presence. The phrase "supremely happy with You forever" speaks to the idea that the only source of supreme happiness that can be eternal, sustained, and unchanging is relationship with our Creator.

We were always intended to be "with" God. Titus 1:2 tells us that eternal life was promised "before the world began." When we step into eternity, everything changes, especially our relationship with God. Having originally been created to have face-to-face relationship with Him, in the next life this state of being is restored. Because our relationship with Him will be as it was originally intended to be, we will experience—without any barriers or distortions—the perfect love He has always had for us. We will know supreme happiness as we finally fulfill the purpose for which we were meant—to fully and completely worship the One who gave us life and in whose image we were created.

We will be supremely happy with God because the whole order of life as we have known it will be changed. Because God's kingdom is perfect, sin cannot exist in it. Revelation 21:27 (NIV) tells us that "nothing impure will ever enter it." We will be supremely happy because we will never again experience the negative consequences of sin. Revelation 21:4 says that there will be no tears, sorrow, crying, pain, or death. Having experienced all of these over the course of my life, it is hard to even conceive of how exhilarating it will feel to have them removed. No losses to grieve. No funerals to attend. No cancer diagnoses to face. No handicaps to endure. No broken relationships to mourn. No character defects to be removed. No tears to shed concerning the hurt inflicted by my shortcomings. No frustration to feel concerning misplaced attempts to control others. No regret to ponder concerning poor choices. Quite simply it will be, as Paul described it, "the kingdom of light" (Colossians 1:12 NIV). What a complete contrast to the "kingdom of heaviness" under which we are presently operating.

In addition to this, the curse that accompanied the sinful fall of the human race and brought deterioration to all of God's creation will be removed (Revelation 22:3). We will know supreme happiness, because in the absence of this curse the way in which we relate to others will be fundamentally altered. The change in our relationships will extend far beyond simply being reunited with our loved ones, which is what we typically think of when we imagine the next life. Paul discussed the idea that in heaven we would be able to see everything with perfect clarity (1 Corinthians 13:12). With the curse of sin removed, the distorted images that we have developed concerning others will be corrected. We will be able to know and appreciate people as the "wonderfully made" individuals God originally created them to be before sin scarred human hearts and distorted personalities (Psalm 139:14 NASB). Regardless of what serious issues might have clouded our relationships in this world, in the next life reconciliation will be the new order of things. We will never again need to work on forgiving others. Being in the presence of Jesus, the One who willingly purchased our forgiveness, we will finally comprehend the all-inclusive cost of our being forgiven, which will enable us to extend forgiveness freely and completely to others. The misunderstandings of the past will be understood. We won't hold grudges. Jealousy, selfishness, personality conflicts, and power struggles will never again block our ability to love others.

I will be supremely happy because I will be able to fully comprehend my identity in Christ. That identity qualifies me to be a member in good standing of the family of God. Identity in Christ means that I qualify on the basis of what He has done rather than what I have done. In fact, there is no other way into the kingdom of supreme happiness except on this basis. Jesus said, "I am the way, the truth, and the life. No one can come to the Father except through me" (John 14:6). My lifetime struggle to overcome my character defects will be finished and I will finally possess the character of Christ. With those defects behind me, I will understand completely what it means to be redeemed.

In heaven, I will never again identify myself as an alcoholic, addict, or codependent. Addiction won't exist and there will be no need for recovery. During the last supper Jesus shared with His disciples, as He gave them a portion of the wine He told them that He would not have another drink until the day when all believers sat down and drank together at a heavenly banquet, commemorating the fulfillment of the kingdom of God (Mark 14:25). Although for different reasons, Jesus has been abstinent just as I have been. But one day in heaven, I will sit down at His banquet table and join Him in drinking a celebratory toast. I will do this without fear of negative consequences or relapse because I will be completely free from the addictions caused by sin. I will be supremely happy, not because

I can drink again, but because I am completely and eternally free from the compulsion of sin. It is no wonder that the Bible paints a picture of our future freedom as being like that of young calves leaping for joy after having been released from the confinement of a stall (Malachi 4:2).

Now all of the above would be enough to inspire supreme happiness, but there is even more. There will be rewards and treasures waiting for us when we get there. I once heard someone say, "You can't take anything from this life with you, but you can send a few things ahead." The way that we create such a "savings account" for the next life is by earnestly seeking God (Hebrews 11:6), which is just what we are attempting to do by living a life surrendered to His will. All that surrendering with which we struggled during our recoveries will one day be worth something more than simple character growth here on earth. It will translate into tangibles in heaven. Our diligent attempts to "accept hardship as a pathway to peace" will qualify us for the title "overcomer." In the book of Revelation, which talks about the life to come, Jesus mentions eight times the various rewards which people "who overcome" will receive (Revelation 2:7–3:22) Right conduct, good deeds, generosity, and humility are just a few of the behaviors which Scripture says will be rewarded. Because our diligent efforts to practice the principles of the Serenity Prayer result in behaviors which are rewarded in heaven, we have a lot to look forward to.

When it comes to the next life, First Corinthians 2:9 says, "No eye has seen, no ear has heard, and no mind has imagined what God has prepared for those who love him." And therein lies the challenge for those of us looking ahead to supreme happiness—it is difficult to adequately comprehend the incomparable gift that God has in store for us because we have never experienced it. In this life, we experience moments of happiness which are fleeting and circumstantial. None of us have ever experienced living in a constant, unchanging state of happiness. The word *supreme* means greatest, utmost, ultimate, extreme, highest, or final.[43] Supreme happiness cannot be measured. There is nothing that approximates it. We cannot relate to the concept of eternity either. Some days it seems to me like it takes an eternity for my computer to load! Nor is there a reference point for the wonder of meeting God. The closest example I can think of would be meeting the president, or having an audience with the queen—and those are not even in the same ballpark.

As wonderful as the prospect of being supremely happy with God forever is, the prayer reminds me that it doesn't happen until "the next" life. In other words, we have to wait for this promise to be realized. While I am waiting around, doing my best to live one day at a time, it is easy to lose sight of eternity. Living with "forever" in mind is important because it has the potential to dramatically influence my "today." That familiar recovery slogan—"How important is it?"—takes on a whole new meaning in light of eternity. Knowing that treasures and rewards can be waiting for me influences the decisions I make regarding how I live my life today. Keeping eternity in mind helps me to reconsider my priorities and inspires me to seek God's will in my actions. It adds another dimension of accountability to my journey of recovery. Recognizing the value God places on overcoming obstacles, and the rewards that await those who do, inspires me to persevere in practicing the principles contained in the Serenity Prayer.

Realizing that supreme happiness is intended for the next life, not the present life, helps me to curb my unrealistic desires and expectations. Too often the pursuit of supreme happiness ends up being the pursuit of "things." Because "things" are dead, they can't impart life or happiness. Ecclesiastes 2:26 indicates that God gives happiness, wisdom, and joy to people who please Him by living according to His principles. Happiness in this life is a by-product of pleasing God; it is not something that can be acquired by chasing "things."

There is a wonderful Scripture found in Ecclesiastes 3:11 which says, "God has made everything beautiful for its own time. He has planted eternity in the human heart, but even so, people cannot see the whole scope of God's work from beginning to end." We long for eternal life. It is one of those deep desires of the heart that reflects the image of our eternal Creator, and that remains frustrated in this life as we wait for the next. All that waiting is a lot like the experience of Abraham, who walked away from his comfortable, affluent home to live in a tent while waiting for God's promises to be fulfilled. The Bible says that he was "confidently looking forward to a city with eternal foundations, a city designed and built by God" (Hebrews 11:10). Abraham's hope was a future hope, just like ours. As we follow the example of this great patriarch by looking forward in faith to the inheritance of supreme happiness awaiting us in the future, how fortunate we are to have the truths of the Serenity Prayer to guide us into serenity for today and hope for tomorrow.

One of these days I will be going on a one-way trip to the ultimate kingdom of happiness—the kingdom of God. I will be ushered into His very presence—not for a handshake or photo op or a few minutes of small talk, but for eternity. The hope King David expressed in his familiar Psalm will be realized, and I will "live in the house of the Lord forever" (Psalm 23:6). At long last I will arrive at my real home, and for the first time in my life I will feel fully alive, completely whole, and entirely at peace. One day at a time, I am another day closer. One moment at a time, I move another step closer.

In the meantime, until that day arrives and for all the moments in between, I am just living serenity.

"And Supremely Happy with You Forever in the Next" and Me

One of my favorite memories of my childhood was when I would come home from school to find a plate of homemade cookies sitting on the kitchen counter. My mother baked the best chocolate chip cookies in the world, and to this day whenever I smell cookies baking I am reminded of home. There's just something comforting about the idea of home. I guess that is why I have a sign on the bookshelf in my family room that reads: "There's no place like home." To me those words aren't just a catchy phrase from a famous Judy Garland film—they are truth.

And yet the reality is that my real home is not in this world. As I approach my sixties, the idea that heaven is my real home takes on a relevance that it lacked when I was younger. As I move through what I consider my "twilight years," heaven has lost the distant-future, fairy-tale-like quality it once had, and instead become a reality that I am rapidly approaching at what now seems like light speed! The majority of people of faith whom I loved and looked up to over the course of my lifetime are now waiting there, making heaven seem more familiar and homelike than ever. Yet perhaps the biggest influence on my change of perception has been the process of recovery itself. Practicing the truths of the Serenity Prayer as well as the twelve steps has helped me to realize how damaging the effects of sin have been to me personally, and as a result of this insight has produced in me a longing for the freedom of heaven that I could not have otherwise grasped.

I used to think of heaven exclusively in terms of what would be there rather than what would not be there. Having been taught about heaven in Sunday school, I had imagined for years the beauty of the crystal sea, the blinding shimmer of the streets of gold, and the lustrous radiance of the "pearly" gates. Family members refer to me as the "glitter queen" because of my tendency toward wanting to embellish everything I see with the sparkly stuff. So the thought of all those glittering objects alone is enough to generate supreme happiness in this crafter's heart! Yet until recovery, I had never stopped to consider that what wouldn't be there offered the possibility of just as much happiness. With the "*dis*-ease" of sin gone, in the next life I will live in a state of ongoing serenity. I won't have to work at serenity, as the "soul rest" promised by Jesus will be my natural state of being. Because I will at last be complete and whole—physically, mentally, emotionally, and spiritually—the neediness which fueled my behavior in this life will cease to exist, and I will never again have to ask myself, "What's wrong with you?" And because I will be "with" God, I will never again struggle with questions designed to figure out or make sense of His will for me. In heaven the slogan "keep it simple" will be realized, and my sole purpose will be to lovingly worship my God.

As I have matured spiritually, I have come to understand what was impossible to understand when I was younger: that this world may bring moments of joy, success, and well-being, but it can never bring supreme happiness; that degree of joy can only be realized when I am physically in the presence of my Lord and Savior. When I was young, long before the advent of computers and email, it was popular to have "pen pals" from another part of the country or world with whom a long-distance friendship could be developed and maintained. Having a relationship with Christ during this life has been a little bit like having a spiritual pen pal. The relationship has been rewarding, but the lack of physical proximity has certainly made it challenging and left me longing for more.

Restoration of relationships is by far one of the aspects of my heavenly home that I most look forward to. The perfect unity found in the next life will mean that the discord that hindered my earthly relationships will not exist in heaven. As pointed out earlier in this book, my relationship with my earthly father was riddled with fear and misunderstanding. Because my father died when I was in my early twenties, we never had the opportunity to resolve those difficulties. The only resolution I have experienced is that associated with learning forgiveness through the practice of my Christian faith. It will bring supreme happiness to finally experience a perfectly repaired and restored relationship and to relate to him in ways that my age, understanding, and the limitations of sin precluded. I do hope that, after Jesus, he is the first person I meet.

Someday, I will arrive at my real home, and it will be ever so much more comforting than a plate of warm chocolate chip cookies on the kitchen counter after school because Jesus will be there to greet me. And I will be supremely happy when I hear Him say, “Welcome home.”

"And Supremely Happy with You Forever in the Next" and You

1. Are you hopeful about your future? Why or why not?

____

____

____

____

2. How can anticipating "supreme happiness" influence your attitude today? How does knowing that you have a "rich inheritance" affect your attitude today?

____

____

____

____

3. What negative consequences of sin will you be supremely happy to have removed?

____

____

____

____

4. How might your relationships with others change with the curse of sin removed?

____

____

____

____

5. What do you most look forward to with regard to heaven?

____

____

____

____

6. How are you creating a "savings account" in heaven?

7. What do these Scriptures reveal about the characteristics of heaven? (Psalm 16:11; Psalm 21:6; Psalm 52:9; Isaiah 35:9-10; Matthew 6:20; Matthew 26:64; Luke 13:29; 2 Corinthians 5:1; Hebrews 12:22)

8. What do these Scriptures indicate will be absent in heaven? (Psalm 5:5; Psalm 101:7; Matthew 6:1; Ephesians 5:5; Revelation 21:4)

9. What reasons does Scripture give for why you will be supremely happy in the next life? (Psalm 41:12; Isaiah 25:6-9; Daniel 7:27; Zechariah 14:9; John 14:2; 1 Corinthians 2:9; Philippians 3:20-21; 1 John 3:2; Jude 24)

10. What characteristics of your future inheritance are revealed in the following Scriptures? (Psalm 37:18; Ephesians 1:13-14; Colossians 1:12; Hebrews 9:15; 1 Peter 1:3-4)

____
____
____
____
____
____
____
____

11. What do the following Scriptures say you will be rewarded for? (Proverbs 19:17; Jeremiah 32:19; Matthew 5:11-12; Matthew 19:29; Matthew 25:34-36; Luke 6:35; Colossians 3:23-24; 2 Timothy 4:7-8; Revelation 21:7)

____
____
____
____
____
____
____
____

12. What idea from this chapter do you plan to put into practice?

____
____
____
____

Chapter Twenty: Amen

When I first began the task of writing this book, I wasn't planning to write this chapter. The original purpose of this book was to guide Christians in recovery into a deeper understanding of the Serenity Prayer through Scripture. But as I was writing it, I realized that in all likelihood someone without a Christian background might read it also. With that possibility in mind, I would be remiss in my convictions if I did not close this book by presenting a clear explanation regarding both the importance of developing a personal relationship with Jesus Christ as well as the process for doing so.

As alluded to in other sections of this book, relationship with Christ was necessitated by the presence of sin. While people were created to be perfect, the free will choice to sin as exercised by Adam and Eve meant that all people from that time forward were born sinful. Because sin separates people from a holy, perfect God, people were doomed to physical and spiritual death until Jesus, through His death and resurrection, bridged the gap between God and people. Paul explained the process this way: "For God made Christ, who never sinned, to be the offering for our sin, so that we could be made right with God through Christ" (2 Corinthians 5:21). Jesus identified Himself as the path to God when He said, "I am the way, and the truth, and the life. No one can come to the Father except through me" (John 14:6).

Through a simple confession of faith in the atoning work of Jesus Christ, we can have relationship with our holy God restored. Similar to any of the changes we make in recovery, the first step in establishing a personal relationship with Jesus involves admitting our need. When we admit that we are sinners in need of a Savior and that the solution for sin is found in Jesus Christ, we find salvation. Romans 10:9-10 explains: "If you confess with your mouth that Jesus is Lord and believe in your heart that God raised him from the dead, you will be saved. For it is by believing in your heart that you are made right with God, and it is by confessing with your mouth that you are saved." This is the simplicity of God's grace which results in both the gift of salvation as well as eternal life. Jesus summarized God's amazing grace when He explained: "For God loved the world so much that he gave his one and only Son, so that everyone who believes in him will not perish but have eternal life. God sent his Son into the world not to judge the world, but to save the world through him" (John 3:16-17).

While salvation is a simple, clear-cut decision, growing in knowledge of Jesus requires effort and commitment, just as it would in any other meaningful relationship. Peter encouraged us to "grow in the grace and knowledge of our Lord and Savior Jesus Christ" (2 Peter 3:18 NASB). There are two important ways that we can do this. One is to begin to read the Bible. Paul explained, "All Scripture is inspired by God and is useful to teach us what is true and to make us realize what is wrong in our lives. It corrects us when we are wrong and teaches us to do what is right. God uses it to prepare and equip his people to do every good work" (2 Timothy 3:16-17). Contained within the pages of the Bible, we find the revelation of God's will and the encouragement of His promises as well as the teachings of Jesus. Jesus described the power of His words as being spirit and life (John 6:63). The more we expose ourselves to His life-engendering words, the deeper our relationship with Him becomes. Many people cite their limited ability to understand the Bible as an excuse to avoid reading it. Considering the number of comprehensible modern language translations of the Bible available to us today, there are many reasonable alternatives to this excuse.

The second important way that we grow in relationship with Jesus is through involvement in a Christ-centered church which focuses on teaching the principles contained in the Bible. Involvement with other Christians is important to our spiritual growth. There are a number of excuses that people present for avoiding church attendance. Chief among these are hypocrisy and "bad" experiences with churches in the past. Churches are a lot like recovery groups; sometimes we have to be willing to attend several different ones until we find the one that best addresses our particular needs. And just like the people in the recovery groups that we attend, some church attendees will be sincerely committed to "walking the talk" while others will lean toward hypocrisy. The Bible tells us that church attendance is beneficial because it gives us the opportunity to encourage one another (Hebrews 10:25). Just as with recovery, our Christian faith is intended to be practiced with others as well as individually. Recovering people recognize the serious risk that isolation poses with regard to personal progress. The same is true with regard to spiritual growth. The isolation that results from lack of church attendance obstructs our ability to receive encouragement from other believers and cuts us off from a helpful source of accountability.

I believe the decision to become a follower of Jesus Christ is the single most important decision we ever make in our lives. It is a decision that, when taken seriously and lived out wholeheartedly, has the power to be life changing. Through relationship with Him, we find not just a bridge to salvation and eternal life, but also a bridge to the serenity we have been so earnestly pursuing.

"Amen" and Me

I can't remember the first time I actually made a decision to turn my life and will over to Jesus Christ. Recalling the fear-oriented gospel of the church of my childhood, I like to joke that I got saved every Sunday whether I needed to or not! I am sure I made many commitments to Christ over the years.

On the other hand, I clearly remember the moment I realized I was a sinner in need of His grace. I was attending a women's retreat where, at the conclusion of the speaker's talk, she encouraged us to begin to confess our shortcomings to God in prayer. There were hundreds of women in the room and we were all praying individually. As I began talking honestly to God about my character defects, I became acutely aware of the extent of my imperfections, as well as the hopelessness of my sinful condition. As my denial continued to lift and I confronted my powerlessness to rescue myself from my inclination to sin, I began to weep. Then, to my embarrassment, I began to sob as I grieved over my own sinful state.

I remember saying repeatedly to God, "I am a wretched, hopeless sinner." And somewhere in the middle of that miserable mantra, God spoke to my heart and said, "Of course you are. I already know that. You need My grace, and I sent My Son for exactly that reason." If I thought I was embarrassed by my sobbing, what happened next was completely unexpected. As the tears subsided, an indescribable joy infused my whole being. As it rose within me, I began to laugh—loudly and without restraint.

Now I assure you that this was not the product of some weird religious cult—it was a fairly conservative group of women. But what was happening to me that afternoon was that for the first time in my life I was connecting on both an emotional and spiritual level to the "amazing" aspect of God's grace. By clearly recognizing the sinful nature of my inner state, and in turn my genuine need for salvation, God's grace ceased to be just a religious concept and instead became a life-changing experience. The extent of my joy may have looked crazy from the outside, but it originated from an overwhelming sense of gratitude for what Christ had made possible for a powerless sinner like me.

It is a fact of my life, although people outside the realm of recovery do not understand this, that even when I do not drink or use, I am still an alcoholic/addict. I am a food addict even when my weight is within a healthy range. And I am a compulsive overspender even when my checkbook balances. Because I am by nature an obsessive compulsive person, I am inclined to become addicted to just about anything I grasp too tightly. When I forget these facts, I run the risk of relapse.

All of these issues are manifestations of falling short of the perfection of God, and as such are sin. The bottom line on all of this is that I am a sinner saved by grace. This will remain a fact of my life until I enter the next one. There will never be a day on this earth that I can claim that I am not a sinner, just as there will never be a day that I can claim I am not an alcoholic. These facts do not cause me to feel burdened or condemned, nor do I perceive them as negative confessions, because fortunately God's grace covers them all, thereby affording me a sense of freedom.

I didn't have to find God's grace, because it found me. While I joke about the church of my childhood, I am seriously grateful for it. Because it was there that I first learned that in spite of my sinfulness, God had a plan to save me. It was a message worth hearing, even if the delivery was somewhat grace challenged. And it most certainly beat the alternative of not having heard the message at all.

"Amen" and You

1. What barriers are preventing you from turning your will and life over to the care of Jesus Christ?

2. If you are serious about wanting relationship with Christ, write a simple prayer admitting your desire and need for Him and asking for His free gift of salvation from sin.

3. Tell another Christian of your prayer for salvation, and ask them to help you find resources to help you on your spiritual journey.

4. What do the following Scriptures tell you about the path to salvation? (John 5:24; John 6:40; Romans 3:22-26; Romans 5:6-8; Romans 10:11-13; 1 Timothy 2:3-4; 1 Peter 3:18; 1 John 1:9; Revelation 3:20)

5. What do the following Scriptures reveal about the importance of God's Word, the Bible? (Psalm 119: 9, 11, 105; John 17:17; Colossians 3:16; 1 Thessalonians 2:13; 2 Thessalonians 2:15; Hebrews 1:3; Hebrews 4:12; James 1:22; 1 Peter 1:23, 25)

6. What does Scripture teach regarding the importance of fellowship among Christians? (Romans 12:4-5; Romans 15:5-6; 1 Corinthians 12:12-27; Ephesians 4:3-4; Philippians 2:1-4; 1 Thessalonians 5:11; Titus 1:9; Hebrews 3:13)

Endnotes

1. Fred Shapiro, "Who Wrote the Serenity Prayer?", *Yale Alumni Magazine*, LXXI, no. 3 (July/August, 2008): 1, accessed March 12, 2013, http://www..archives.yalealumnimagazine.com/articles/2143.
2. "The Elusive Origins of the Serenity Prayer", *Box 459*, 38, no. 4 (August-September, 1992): 1.
3. Ibid.
4. Richard Fox, *Reinhold Niebuhr: A Biography*, (San Francisco: Harper and Row, 1985), 1, 38, 62, 96-98, 11, 195-196.
5. Elisabeth Sifton, *The Serenity Prayer: Faith and Politics in Times of Peace and War* (New York: W. W. Norton and Company, 2003), 18, 292.
6. Fox, *Reinhold Niebuhr*, 290.
7. Sifton, *The Serenity Prayer*, 277, 292-3.
8. Fox, *Reinhold Niebuhr*, 290.
9. Sifton, *The Serenity Prayer*, 293.
10. Shapiro, "Who Wrote the Serenity Prayer?"
11. Stephen Goranson, email communication, June 1, 2013.
12. Fox, *Reinhold Niebuhr*, 291.
13. Fred Shapiro, email communication, March 8, 2012.
14. Stephen Goranson, email communication, June 1, 2013.
15. Heiko A. Oberman, *Luther: Man Between God and the Devil*, translated by Eileen Walliser-Schwarzbart (New Haven: Yale University Press, 1989), 315.
16. "This is my Father's World," 1901, public domain.
17. Lawrence O. Richards, *Richard's Complete Bible Dictionary* (Iowa Falls, IA: World Bible Publishers, Inc., 1973), 940.
18. James Strong, *Strong's Exhaustive Concordance of the Bible* (Peabody, MA: Hendrickson Publishers, Inc., 2007), 1685.
19. Ibid., 1583.
20. Ibid., 1621.
21. Exerpt from NO MAN IS AN ISLAND by Thomas Merton. Copyright ©1955 by The Abbey of Our Lady of Gethsemani and renewed 1983 by the Trustees of the Merton Legacy Trust. Reprinted by permission of Houghton Mifflin Harcourt Publishing Company. All rights reserved.
22. Taken from *Quiet Strength: The Principles, Practices and Priorities of a Winning Life* by Tony Dungy. Copyright © 2007 by Tyndale Momentum. Used by permission of Tyndale House Publishers, Inc. All rights reserved. (Pages 105, 116, 215-216, 295).
23. *Webster's Collegiate Dictionary,* s. v. "courage."
24. Ibid., s. v. "wisdom."
25. Wikiquote contributors, "Wisdom," *Wikiquote,* http://en.wikiquote.org/w/index.php?title=Wisdom&oldid=1540398 (accessed April 19, 2013).

26. Zhe-Yu Chen, et al, "Genetic Variant BDNF (Val 66 Met) Polymorphism Alters Anxiety Related Behavior", *Science* 314, no. 5796 (October 6, 2006): 140.
27. Corrie Ten Boom and John and Elizabeth Sherrill, *The Hiding Place* (New York: Bantam Books, 1971), 202.
28. Wikiquote contributors, "Cesare Pavese," *Wikiquote,* http://en.wikiquote.org/w/index.php?title=Cesare_Pavese&oldid=1504905 (accessed April 19, 2013).
29. *Webster's,* s. v. "enjoy."
30. Strong, *Strong's Exhaustive Concordance,*1548.
31. Ibid., 1493, 1575.
32. Fox, *Reinhold Niebuhr*, x.
33. Strong, *Strong's Exhaustive Concordance*, 1643.
34. *Webster's,* s. v. "accept."
35. *Webster's,* s. v. "tolerate."
36. Strong, *Strong's Exhaustive Concordance*, 1634.
37. Bruce Marchiano, email communication, January 17, 2013.
38. The National Center on Addiction and Substance Abuse at Columbia University, *No Safe Haven: Children of Substance Abusing Parents* (New York: The National Center on Addiction and Substance Abuse at Columbia University, January, 1999), i-ii.
39. Strong, *Strong's Exhaustive Concordance*, 1501.
40. Panagore, Rev. Peter B, *Two Minutes for God* (New York:Simon & Schuster, 2007), 73.
41. *Webster's,* s. v. "surrender."
42. Jerome Irving Rodale, *The Synonym Finder* (Emmaus, PA: Rodale Press, Inc., 1978), 992.
43. Ibid., 1198.

About the Author

Deborah Galasso, RN, MS is a clinical nurse specialist who has worked in the behavioral health field throughout her thirty-five year career. She received her master's degree from Loma Linda University and her certificate in advanced alcohol and drug studies from the University of California, Riverside. Deborah has conducted workshops and educational programs in both the hospital and community settings on a wide range of topics related to addiction recovery. She has served as program leader for the recovery ministry at Centerpoint Church in Colton, California for over twelve years. Visit her website at www.livingserenity.net.

More Titles by 5 Fold Media

The Transformed Life
by John R. Carter
$20.95
ISBN: 978-1-936578-40-5

Personal transformation requires radical change, but your life will not transform until you change the way you think. Becoming a Christian ignites the process of transformation.

In this book, John Carter will teach you that God has designed a plan of genuine transformation for every person, one that goes far beyond the initial moment of salvation. More than a book, this 10 week, 40 day workbook will show you how to change.

Letters from Heaven
The Passion Translation
by Brian Simmons
$12.95
ISBN: 978-1-936578-56-6

Some of the most beautiful and glorious truths of the Bible are found in the letters of the Apostle Paul. Paul's letters are now available in The Passion Translation. Reading through these letters is like having Paul sitting in your living room personally sharing his experience of the power and majesty of God's Word for His people. Be ready to sense the stirring of the Holy Spirit within you as you read Letters from Heaven by the Apostle Paul.

I highly recommend this new Bible translation to everyone.
~ Dr. Ché Ahn, Senior Pastor of HRock Church in Pasadena, CA

Like 5 Fold Media on Facebook, follow us on Twitter!

CPSIA information can be obtained at www.ICGtesting.com
Printed in the USA
BVOW01s0305200114

342306BV00008B/44/P

9 781936 578795